BRAVO

A MEMOIR

BY TERESA BRAVO-CORTINES

Strategic Book Publishing and Rights Co.

Strategic Book Publishing and Rights Co., LLC
USA | Singapore
www.sbpra.com

For information about special discounts for bulk purchases, please contact Strategic Book Publishing and Rights Co., LLC Special Sales, at bookorder@sbpra.net.

ISBN: 978-1-68181-657-9

Chapter One

I guess when one decides to talk about their life, one must come to grips with where will you start. What will you talk about? Do you clean a bunch of it up, do you take some of the gore out of it, or do you just tell it like it is? Take all the pretty out of it and let your book be a tale of how things happen and how your life experiences shape, mold and make up who you are? No matter how tough your life choices have been, they're no comparison for what takes place at the end. Perhaps they're small steps to prepare you for what's to come. I guess this is where I start baring all, being honest with myself and with you, being honest with everybody. I'm letting everybody know what it feels like, what I might be going through, why I'm here, and how I got here.

The first childhood memory I have is me sitting on the side of the bed. It's dark; it's kind of fresh—not cold, just fresh. I keep looking at the shape of something horrific in the darkness. I'm not sure what it is, but for the life of me I don't look away from it. Every now and then I would close my eyes real tight and say a little prayer so that it would give me the courage to continue on looking. Instead I'm just doing the right thing and going right back to sleep. I stared at it for as long as I could, until I drifted off into the night. In the morning I quickly get up and look back at the sheet that had been taunting me the entire night; it's just the antlers.

My dad had gone deer hunting the night before, and he put the deer inside the house to keep the animals away from his meat. He wasn't going to start skinning and cutting until the morning. So putting the deer inside of the house was much safer than leaving the deer outside on the porch. Alongside the deer he had left his rifle, his hunting rifle. He had it cornered it up against the wall. My brother Jose and I thought it would be fun for us to pretend like we knew what we were doing and we tried to load the rifle. My dad caught both of us playing with his rifle and took a nice, hard whooping onto both of us. My mother was screaming in the background, asking him to stop and begging him. Yelling, "Lupe, Lupe, stop! They're just children! Stop! Leave them alone. Stop!"

I don't know where my dad came up with the idea that he should just leather belt my brother and I because we were playing with his gun instead of taking responsibility for leaving the gun on the floor and the ammunition close to it.

I guess this is where I tell you my dad was an absolute punk. He took great pride in being mean, and took great pride in belittling my mother, making her cry, and making us cry. He would hit her because she defended us, and she got in the way of our whooping half the time. Half the time he would just come home drunk and angry. Nothing we said or did was good enough for him, but like all good drunk men, he was also sweet and wonderful and happy, and made you laugh and loved throwing parties. He was the life of the party, and the guy who always had the money to throw the party and kill a pig for the town, kill a cow and a goat, and throw a party. As far as he was concerned, life was a party.

One particular party night he and his sidekick, Rafael, came home. It sounded like they were arguing and exchanges words, big words. My father gave up and just came home and went to bed, and Rafael went home to his wife and family. The following morning my father up and decides to kill a pig. He had this jukebox-like record player contraption that he had hooked up or Jimmy-rigged to some speakers. He could play vinyls on it. He would turn up the music as loud as it could go and play a couple of his *Jilguerillas*, his *Palomas*, all the music he had brought back from the US, all the vinyls and bunch of stereo equipment he needed so he could play his music as loud as he possibly could.

This day was like any other day, with music and friends and light drinking during the day, and partying and kids dressed up looking pretty with bows in their hair, cleaned up for our town to hang out with. Not an unusual Saturday morning. My brother and I used to fight and compete to see who could find the paddle to stir the chicharones with. Whoever found the paddle was the winner of the grand prize, which was the pig tail. I'm not sure why we even liked it, but my brother and I would kill each other for it and duke it out if we had to, but mostly we would compete.

My father would find the tail at the bottom of the *cazuela* and pull it out with this big wooden spoon that we had found for him. It was a bit of a boat row. I guess that's what it looked like, a wooden row. He would take that wooden thing and mix the *chicharones* around, and the sound of the pork and the fat crinkling, the sound of the fire, the sound of my father's music, the sound of the horses in the background, the sound of all of us playing and people talking, and people gossiping were all the stuff that takes place in Little Ranchos, Mexico.

My father traveled between America and Mexico because of his job. He had taken care of the forestry department. Winter times were slow seasons. That meant he could come home and visit his parents, spend money on mom and dad, make sure the farm was running right, and fix roofs and fix fences and make sure his parents' livestock inventory was on point. If they had any missing cows, if anybody owed them money, collecting debts, paying off debts, paying back favors. My father was a very honorable man, very honest, very hard working. Pride was his middle name. His last name was Bravo. I love my last name. I always have.

I always felt like you don't accidently get a name like Bravo. It means "brave." It means "unafraid." I found that throughout the years that it motivated me to stand up straight and keep on marching forward. I felt that if my father wanted me to bow down he wouldn't have given me such a powerful last name.

And now, as I sit here talking into this contraption, I'm dying. According to what the doctors say, "you're dying." I'm not very good at dying I guess. I've seen death, but I'm not very good at dying. I am better at living, I'm better at laughing, and I'm better at smiling and taking it all in stride. When they throw big words at you and chronic diseases, you can't help but take your breath away. When you spend two weeks in the hospital and you realize that you're not that strong person you thought you were two weeks earlier, when you're being tube fed, intubated, all that good stuff, you realize that maybe you're not made of steel. Maybe you are just as the next guy is—scared. Maybe being scared is all right. Maybe being scared means you have some fighting to do, some living to do, some not giving up.

I think that if you stop being afraid you might stop living, because I find that fear, for the most part, has been my driving force —the fear of failing, the fear of not doing enough, the fear of not being fast enough, growing up fast enough. It might have been brought on by the death of my father. I don't remember much about him. I don't remember much. I just remember that he loved me. He took me everywhere he went. I was his pride and joy. I was his little Nina, a name that I carried for over twelve years. Not until I was in middle school did I think Nina was a little immature so then chose Teresa, but for now I am Nina and I'm sitting in a dark room and I'm not afraid. Like all dark rooms, there does come a time when you are very afraid.

The day my father died, I guess it was one of those real beautiful, unafraid, real sunny, perfect days. My brothers and I spent the better part of the day playing in a hill stream that was in front of our house and our grandfather's house. We were surrounded by family. Our grandfather to the right, we were in the middle, my uncle to the left, and uncles across the stream. So everybody knew everybody. Everybody was related. They were all first cousins and very close friends who'd been there fifty years, which still made them family. My first cousins and us played together all day every day in the little stream. We used to go play with tin cans and catch crawdads and try to see if we could get mom to cook them for us. She always refused, but we always caught tiny little crawdads. After she refused to cook them, we would throw them right back into the stream, because we weren't going to cook them ourselves.

Saturday morning, dad's killed a pig, has a bunch of friends over, got his music going full blast, then Rafael shows up. And when Rafael shows up, we were happy to see him. We thought he was my dad's friend. He was, I think, our uncle. So we greeted him and we were happy to see him. As he walks off towards my father, we continue playing in the stream. Out of nowhere this helicopter just comes out. I did not even know. We had never seen one. We had never heard one. I now know it's a helicopter, but as a child we thought it was a big, loud, scary birdhawk-type animal. My younger brother Lupe panicked every time he saw one, and he would just scream out of control and run towards dad, who would always punish him for being afraid and get him to come right back to playing in the stream with us. We couldn't comfort him much. We were just as afraid. We just didn't go running to Dad and tell him.

My cousins eventually told us to just not be afraid. It was just a big bird in the sky, and birds never fell out of the sky, so that wouldn't fall out of the sky either. So we just went along with that and we were good.

Then my father called us up to get cleaned up and dressed up so that his friends could come over for dinner—and, of course, drinking and singing and carrying on. It then comes time for my father and his friend to head off into town for a normal night of binge drinking and over drinking, then coming home to their wives and laying down the law at home, I guess.

My father was famous for making my mom sing in front of his drunk group of bastards. He just found that it was amazingly funny to make my mother sing as he's putting a gun to her temple. You would think his friends would have a problem watching their friend force his wife to sing at gunpoint, but they pretended like it wasn't anything. They pretended like it was just normal. So I suppose they did the same thing to their wives. I don't know. I was just a child looking at them and hating it. I hated every single one of them for making my dad drink.

We thought that my dad was wonderful until he drank. Once he got a few beers in him, that wonderful dad that would take you to the market and buy you anything was just this absolute monster. He took it out on everybody, including his parents. He was the youngest of three, and because he took off to the US and brought home dollars it made him better than them somehow or another. It made him better than a lot of the folks in that little poor town, because he was able to accomplish a lot with a little. He was able to buy large pieces of land. He was able to plant corn, beans, and whatever else they grew in that little town. Cucumbers, pumpkins, and squash were particularly bountiful, but mainly beans and corn and a lot of tropical fruit. My brother and I were in charge of bringing them lunch on horseback, so my mother was in charge of making lunch.

My mom, believe it or not, was not much of a cook—wasn't then, isn't now. She never really enjoyed cooking. She had to pack a lunch for him and his crew, and water for him and his crew, and beer most of the time, or just a big bottle of liquor. I'm not sure what it was. I'm going to assume tequila, but send us off with drinks and food, and our horses knew where to go. They knew every turn; they knew every bend. We were just responsible for pretty much keeping an eye on each other and talking to one another along the way.

My dad was really nice. Every time we showed up with lunch he was very, very nice. He would always help us off the horse and get us to sit down and ask us to eat with him and his friends. He would get my brother and I to take turns sitting on his lap eating with him. I remember taking his hat off. He wore this handkerchief tied around his head all the time, I imagine to catch the sweat. I remember I would smell it and I loved the smell of his sweat.

I would look into his beautiful eyes. His eyes were a hazel/green/blue. I'm not exactly sure, but they used to call him "Cat Eyes" because his eyes used to change. His hair was a little on the long side, very light and curly. A tall, slender man, he had very defined cheek bones. He was a very stern man most of the time, but there was times he was just as soft as can be, and he always had a surprise for us. He always had something he had found for us. Mostly it was gag gifts. He would clip his toenails and save them and tell you they were *chicharones*. He would call them our little snacky snacks.

One time he thought he would be funny and he had a surprise for me, and he comes out with a stick—and this stick was this huge snake, a huge snake, especially to a five-year-old. The snake was still moving a little bit because he had just killed it. It was still twitching, but it was dead.

He would ask me to bite it. He would be like "¡Muerdelo, nena! ¡Muerdelo, mija!" As I would go towards the snake to take a bite from it, he would pull it away and say, "No, no, no, caca." He would ask me again to bite it, and I would go towards the snake to bite it, and he would be like, "No, no, no, caca." Then he would eventually throw it into the field and tell me, "You're not supposed to play with those, sweetheart. Those are venomous."

I used to think, *Well then why in the heck did you want me to bite it?* But he thought he was a jokester. One of my younger brothers is a lot like him. He is just the class clown and just the jokester. He's just the funny guy, my brother Sal. One of my favorite people in the world too.

We would spend the day with him in the field, and we would watch the men take this stick, a Y-shaped stick, and flip the corn over so that it would be dry on both sides, and flip the beans over so they would dry on both sides. My father would always tell us that moldy corn or beans are worthless. So that was his drying method. They used to put these sheets of cloth or burlap underneath, and I think they shake it and catch the beans after it was dry. I'm not positive, but I think that's what they used to do.

I guess my brother and I were pretty familiar with horses, cows, and the animals around our yard, and the chickens and whatnot. So riding into town was just normal for us. Taking care of mom was normal for us. This one time my mother found this iguana inside our house. I guess we had told her there was this one iguana inside our house. Out of nowhere she whipped out a gun and just started shooting at the iguana underneath one of our beds. I remember we thought she was a superstar, this superhero. She was just this bad-ass woman. Now we realize my mom's pretty short. She's only four feet six, weighs one hundred pounds. So she's not much of a woman, but back then we thought she was a heaping giant.

I guess that's the memories I have of her and dad. She was this person who'd take care of us in the daytime, and then in the dark time she would pray to us. Our house was not lit with electricity, so when the candles went out it was time to sit in the dark and talk, or sit in the dark and pray and ask her where Dad was and know that he just wasn't coming home.

The day he died was like no other day. Typical dad, typical day, going to town and find my dad drunk, persuade him to get home, only to have him shot halfway along his ride home. My dad got shot in the back of the neck by his friend whom he had gone drinking with for years and years and years, his loyal drinking companion, his right-hand man. I had no clue that Rafael would be the man that took his life.

As my dad laid in his own blood, the sound of the coyotes or wolves or something was the eeriest sound, where your hair just stood on end, your arm, back, and neck hairs. The sound of my grandfather crying, and sound of the ladies coming to visit my mother crying, was eerie too. Then they forced my mother to wear this black thing over her head, this black lace see-through thing. I don't know, but that made it even scarier to see her moping around in the dark with this thing and dressed in black, as if it was some type of punishment if anything.

When my father died he didn't leave us much. He left us animals. He had a lot of livestock. We had our house that was paid for. We had land, but my mom only had what she knew best, which was her family in America. So she had to come back home and pluck us away from everything we knew.

My father was put to rest less than two days after he got shot, but I remember thinking he was sleeping. I wondered why he was laying in a cot in the middle of this bar with everybody around him just looking at him. So I was wondering what the heck he was doing sleeping, but then I looked underneath the cot and noticed that there was this metal, white tin bowl underneath his head catching every drop of blood. I remember smelling it. I remember getting way deep down in it, and then just smelling the smell of my dad's blood. Even though I wasn't supposed to, I kind of dipped my finger in it and just smelled it, and I knew my dad was dead when I could smell what smelt like deer. I remember when he brought deer home that we had the smell of blood while he took care of the meat while he skinned it, while he gutted it, while he cut it open and whatnot.

As I watched him lay there peacefully, I guess I knew I was never going to see him again. I was too young to know that, but deep down inside I knew. I knew that my dad was gone, but then he looked so peaceful I wasn't convinced until I saw blood. To this day, the smell of blood takes me back to that day. It takes me back to that day of the deer in the dark room, to the smell of my father dying, to wondering what the heck he was doing displayed for everybody in town to see. Why wasn't he someplace safer I guess? I don't know. Why wasn't he put away? Now I understand that that's how they lay people out to rest in Mexico, because I've only known what I've known. You buy a casket. You go to a funeral home and that's where you see a body, if you want to see a dead body, not a cot in the middle of town at the bar he drank at, the bar that would coincidently be the last place he spent his waking moments.

The day my mom buried my dad, I remember looking up at her and looking at her arms and noticed that she still had bruise marks from my dad whipping her the day he died. The day my dad died my mom pleaded with him, she begged him not to go into town, that she had had a horrible, awful, vivid dream about murky water or dirty water. I guess in her psyche, of all psyches, she always knew that if she dreamt with dirty water, not to put aside the fact that she had seen an owl evening. According to Mexican legend, an owl was a sign of death, according to my mother, according to old wives' tales, and followed by a bad dream. He didn't care about the dream, but he just took it upon himself to whoop her for telling him that she had had a bad premonition. As she was burying him, you couldn't help but notice the bruise marks still left on her arms. Even after my father was dead, he had not only left my mother pregnant with my younger brother Miguel, but he had also left her bruise marks and then a whole bunch of mouths to feed.

CHAPTER TWO

My mom contacts her family and we come back home, and I thank my Aunt Nancy for that. My Aunt Nancy made sure that we made it home safely. She put up with us the entire trip home. It wasn't a flight home. It was a drive home in my Aunt Nancy's red station wagon, which happened to be the most fun place to travel in for a while. We got to see a bunch of beautiful parts with our road trip. Then we got to meet her children, and we got along fantastic with them. We came back to Yakima, Washington, where my mom's family is from, and we have to somehow or another squeeze into my grandmother's house on Third Street. We learned real quickly how tight a house can be when you're not welcome in it, because the last thing we were was welcome.

We quickly got kicked out. Unfortunately it was the middle of winter. We had spent about three months too many at my grandmother's house, and she was afraid her landlord was going to kick her out. About the third or fourth month of living for free in my grandmother's tight little apartment, my aunt decides to tell my mom that she has to make like Mike and beat it. She's got to hit the road with all of us, not taking into consideration that younger brother Miguel was only a few weeks old at the time.

My mother had taken us to this garage right beside the apartments that my grandmother lived at. It was an old, abandoned

11

shack of some sort. She curled us all in there, found newspapers, and built a bed out of newspaper and old clothes that people had left behind. She put a bunch of clothes together, tied a bunch of mats together, and covered us all up and told me to watch my brothers, that she had to go find us a place to live. Be it as my younger brother was a newborn, probably only three or four weeks old, he was bundled up best. My mom found, of all things, in that old shack an old space heater, which she was able to plug in and get going, and we were able to keep the shack somewhat warm while she walked the streets of Yakima trying to find us a place to live.

She made it to this place called Gary's Red Apple Market, which is no longer there. I guess there's a hotel there now, but on Ninth and Yakima I think, Eighth and Yakima, but there was a little market. Probably the first little market where a lot of Mexicans hung out was that Roy's IGA on Sixth Street. My mother went to this market, and she said she felt so helpless. She didn't know what to do. All she knew is that she had to find us a place to live, a job, and get back to us in that cold shack as soon as possible, get us food, if anything just food for the night, food for the morning. She didn't know anything about the mission. She didn't know anything about welfare, and I think she was determined not to put us on welfare, because she never did.

She bumps into this lady who is at Gary's Red Apple Market to sell Avon. She's not even there to grocery shop, but she is the Avon lady. I can't think of her name right this second, but she also, ironically, rented rooms, bedrooms for young men that came and picked in the orchards. So they were paying 300 to 400 dollars for a bedroom and didn't have to rent an entire house. So this lady was nice enough to let my mom and all of us move into a room, not a house, but into a room that she was renting that came with a bed. I think it was a queen-size bed, because we all slept on it. It had a little two-eye burner stove that was attached onto this piece of wood. It wasn't a real stove. It was just a two-burner, plug-in contraption stove, and a little fridge on the floor. It made it so we could live there for a few months until my mother got a job and found us a better place to live. For then it worked out.

The Avon lady and her husband, I can't think of his name either, who had Parkinson's, lived in the main house and rented off the rest of the rooms of the main house. The house was kitty-corner from Roy's IGA and sort of kitty-corner to Gary's Red Apple Market. So there was a store behind us and a store in front of us, sort of, and the lady lived in the middle. I think it was on Seventh Street. Like I said, we lived there for a few months. It seemed like night and day, but we loved being there for a few months, and she babysat us while my mom found a job. She and her husband would charge my mom to feed us, but then what they would give us was their leftovers. I remember them giving us bad beans, to where my brothers and I got really sick because the beans were past rotten. She would give us a role of donuts. We didn't care. As far as we were concerned she was giving us caviar and sushi and all the great meals that great people deserve, I guess.

We were getting fed and my mom was getting a job, and that's all that mattered, and we had a warm place to sleep. We didn't have to stay at Grandma's anymore. We didn't have to hear my aunt insult our mother. It would make my mother cry all the time. My mother cried all the time. Half the time I wondered if she was crying because my dad had died, or if she was crying because of her living circumstance. Unfortunately, it was probably a combination of the two, mixed in with she had all of these kids to take care of and feed, and she had no clue how to do it.

My mom had a second-grade education, didn't know how to drive a car, and had never worked. She was taken by my father from Porterville, California, when she was only twelve years old. So when my mom was twelve, she was an adult living in Porterville, California, Fresno, and Tulare. He eventually took her to Mexico, where he would die, and then we come back to Yakima, Washington, where her family lives. There we come to find out real quickly how tough it is to live without your father, and not just because you need him financially and emotionally, but you need him to fend off the other people that are your family who are supposed to embrace you and maybe feel a little compassion, not only for us but for my mother.

My mother had gone through hell and back, and nobody had defended her. Nobody came to her aid. As a matter of fact, somebody did come to her aid. When my mother was pregnant with my older brother Jose, she went to see a gynecologist, a doctor, who would eventually call the police on my father while my father was waiting in the doctor's waiting area. The doctor was beside himself when he figured out that my mother, at twelve years old, was pregnant. So the doctor called the authorities. The authorities came, arrested my father, and took my mother to the juvenile system in California, but they eventually released her when she was close to giving birth to my brother, released her out of fear that she would have a child in the juvenile system; they were not adapted for that. So they give my mother back to my father. Actually, they gave my mother back to her uncle, who would eventually give her back to my father. My father would eventually take us to Mexico because he did not want us here. He didn't want to go to prison for impregnating my mother.

My mother goes back to my father, my father goes back to Mexico, and eventually dies in Mexico. We end up back in America. We end up kicked out to the streets, all this within the first six months of my father dying. Kicked out into the streets in mid-winter, then find a place to live where two adult people think it's okay to feed us their leftovers, their rotten food, but it's the best they could do with what they had at the time. It's the best my mother could do with what she had at the time. We eventually move into another lady's house on Third Street, right in front of what is now the Yakima Police Department. The lady's name was Lonya Salut. That's what we called her—Lonya Salut. She took us all in to live in her house with her and her one son, Valdo.

This lady would pamper us. She would make us homemade tortillas. She took my mother in as her daughter. She disciplined her as her daughter. She yelled at her and gave her advice and critiqued her as if she was her daughter. My mother and her had like a love/hate relationship, but she was wonderful to us. Even though she was very disciplined and very rigorous in the way she did things, we were very structured, and she was very to the point and didn't care about hurting your feelings, which made it kind of nice because she was a real person. She treated us like family. She treated us like we were really her family, and that made it easy for us to adapt into our new environment.

We went to school from her house for at least a couple of years. I remember being in the first grade and in the second grade living with her. So at least for a couple of years she took us in, and I would eventually meet my second-grade teacher, Ms. Vevins, who inspired me to learn the language and learn it quick. She was also a teacher in Mexico before she was a teacher in the US, so she spoke the language and understood the culture. She understood us and she understood my mom, and even understood maybe why my mother's family had turned their back on her, because she understood the culture.

She gave my mother good advice, but the advice she always gave her was: educate yourself, learn faster, even when you're learning fast or not learning fast enough. So my mother learned to drive real quickly. She also learned that she had to fend for herself real quickly, and that no one was going to come out and help her take care of us. It was up to her. So she learned to take care of us. She learned to take care of us quick. She wasn't great at it, because, looking back, there were a lot of things that she could have done differently. But I'm sure every parent would say the same thing about their parenting: when we look back we learn from our mistakes and that we could do it a little bit differently.

I just appreciate everything my mother did. I appreciate her great sacrifice, because my father left her with all of us. She didn't make the choice to have all of us on her own. The other 50-percent partner was gone, and that would be my father. He left her destitute. He left her to fend for herself. He left her to fend for all of us and left her without the skills to do it. It was unfair. It was unfair to my mother and it was unfair to us. It was unfair to us to take on the responsibility of being our father and making a conscious decision to not be there for us.

Lonya Salut became our adopted aunt, grandmother, and friend. She even took us to church. She was very Catholic, so she took us to church and forced us to learn right and wrong. She disciplined if we needed it. Now I'm thankful for everything she's ever done for us. Thank God I've gone back and I've thanked her myself for being there for me, for being there for my siblings, for being there for my mother. It wasn't her obligation to do it, yet she did it. Now that she's passed, I believe she's in heaven. I believe she's looking down on us, and she's still taking care of us, as well as my father. I believe that maybe in his passing he could do a better job of taking care of us from heaven than he did on earth, because we've all turned out okay. We've all turned out okay. Not the greatest, but okay.

My third-grade teacher was also a Mexican American. Luis Corbero was a wonderful inspiration. He helped my mother out, and he talked her through a lot of things that she needed to learn, and inspired myself and my brothers that we could become teachers if that's what we wanted to do. So far we had two great Mexican American teachers that told us that you can be anything you want if you try hard enough. So here I am in the third grade doing well with my English, learning that I wanted to speak English because I wanted to know what everybody else was saying. I didn't want them talking about me behind my back and I wasn't in on it. I wanted to be in on the joke. I wanted to know what other people thought. I wanted to see it through somebody else's eyes.

Ms. Vevins invited me to spend a summer with her and her family when I was in the third grade. That was probably one of the best experiences I've had, because her husband was white and she was Mexican. That allowed me to look into this household that was made up of two equal parts that were completely different but tied into everything that I would become in the future. It tied into me believing that everything that was attainable was attainable. This lady met this guy in Mexico, falls in love, and he brings her back to America. She becomes a teacher in America and he's a successful businessman. It was doable.

The more I spoke English, the more people relied on me to start translating. So I was that young kid translator that everybody depended on. As far back as I could remember, I translated for my mom's friends, translated for the neighbors. If there was a discussion to be had, I wanted to be in on it, because I didn't want them to get the short end of the stick because they didn't understand the language. So by the time I was in the fourth or fifth grade, I knew I wanted to be an attorney. I knew beyond the shadow of a doubt that's what I wanted to be, and I felt that I had it in me to be one.

I was a busy child in school. I participated in drill team, basketball, patrol, kitchen, *bailables*, and square dancing. I was involved in everything. I wanted to soak it all in. I wanted to be a part of the big picture. I wanted to be accepted, and the only way I could be accepted, I felt like, was to speak the language. I felt that our family had rejected us because we were fresh off the boat, because we didn't speak the language, because we didn't understand certain things they already knew. Nobody had taught us. We only knew what we knew. My first English word was *refrigerator*. My second English word was *suitcase*. So, either I was hungry and wanted to pack and go, or I was always going to have food in the fridge and always have a suitcase ready.

You think about what you said first and why you thought of that first. It's just one of the little fragments that makes you, you; one of the little colors that paints the picture of you. I don't think we're that far separated. There are people who are strong and people who are weak, people that are loud, people that are meek. I think we're very closely related, but we like to focus in on our differences so much so that we don't see how we're all intertwined, how we're all closely related, how that second-grade teacher influenced me to be something other than I was, how that third-grade teacher also influenced me and added to the foundation on what the second-grade teacher had taught, which was that it can be done.

My sixth-grade teacher, Mr. Padilla, was a bit of the second part of the picture. He looked Mexican but didn't speak Spanish, and I had a hard time with that. I had a hard time understanding why he was brown like I was. His parents were Mexican. I didn't understand, although he was of Mexican descent, how he didn't speak Spanish. I didn't come to find out until now that the language, no matter how strong it is, washes down second and third generation down because we have to adapt. Whether we want to adapt or don't want to adapt, we have to adapt to better our jobs, to better our education, to better our circumstances, to move out of the hood, to move to the nicer side of town, to have the nicer cars, to talk about annuities and life savings and retirement plans and 401(k)s, versus we're going to work until we can't work anymore and we'll retire at sixty-five or seventy but unable to do anything else with a very small savings account.

That's how I lived my life until I was about ten. We moved into this house on Tenth Street behind a tavern. That's where most of my influence was, living behind a tavern. Living behind a tavern taught us a lot of things. First it taught me that I loved living in a house, because it was the first house we lived in. I loved having a house. We loved having a backyard, a side yard, alley access. We loved that there was a tavern next to our house, because we were very busy children. And as busy children do, we got into some trouble. Also, since we were a big family, we hung out with other big families like the Gutierrezes who lived down the block from us. We played with the Rodriguezes. We played with big families. We had a friend we called "Color Tile" because we used to laugh about his clothing and the various colors of clothing he wore that never matched. So his nickname was Color Tiles, like the Color Tiles store in Yakima. Any tile, any color you could find, you could find on Color Tiles. We had friends that were poorer than we were, where they made us understand we were not as poor as you could get.

We had a friend who lived in Yakima by Jefferson Street who had no running water and no power. His father used to power up their house with a car battery that was attached to some wires that was attached to a light bulb, and that's how they got power. We had functioning power in our house.

My mother worked, so we knew that every Saturday she got paid. Every Saturday we would get sweet cereal. Sunday was church, and Monday it was back to work and back to school. My mom splurged on Saturdays. We had the good stuff and we would try to eat it all the same day. We were bad that way. We didn't get it often, so when we did get it we wanted to just go through it that same day. All seven of us around the table fighting for that one toy inside the cereal box. Half the time it was survival of the fittest. Whoever was strongest, whoever cried the loudest got Mom's attention and forced her to give it to them—that was my sister Virginia. We challenged each other—that would be me. I always accepted the challenge, and my brothers always saw to it that I got the worst challenges. I would have to eat a hot pepper, a handful of dry peppers or something gross, a gross concoction that they would come up with, and I would always be first man in line raising my hand saying, "I want the toy, so I'm willing to do what I've got to do."

We used to play this game called capping, which we used to come up with a cap, and a cap was like a "your momma" joke or "your momma's so this" or "your momma's so that." We used to come up with cap lines or go downstairs in the basement of our house and rap, because rap was starting during that time and we thought we were Flow'etic or whatever, and we thought we were Tupac before Tupac was around.

We were down in the basement recording over a tape that we found that we shouldn't have found, a cassette tape. It was made up of Mexican rap, and it wasn't really rap. It was *corridos*, which were Mexican songs re-sung in a very graphic, nasty sort of way. It was guys talking about the girlfriends being sluts and about the girlfriends hanging out in the bars, getting shot up because they're out barhopping. We added our own mix, because there was this one aunt that we had, my mother's cousin, she was a bit of a ho, as we called her, or a floozy. She was a male magnet. Men loved her. She had a twenty-seven-inch waist and thirty-eight-inch hips. Before Kim Kardashian was Kim Kardashian, there was my mom's cousin, Tia Teresa Nalgas. Her name was "Aunt Ass." Her ass was so big you could hitch a ride on it. She was famously known for that. All the men in the Race Track Tavern loved her because she could open a room by whipping her hips from side to side. I guess she was a fun gal.

We would go down in the basement and sing rap songs about her, until my mother found the cassette. My mom had no clue we were up to this rap game, and one day she somehow or another found it and they decided, I think, to listen to this vulgarity themselves. They had no clue we were on it, but it was their own little version of their Mexican rap. So shame on them for having it I guess. So they listened to their rap cassette with my brother Salvador and his own little rap additions. Me, of course, I had to throw my own little rap versions. My brother Jose, our friend Elvis, our friend Contreras, we all had our little rap version. We thought we were just flow masters. So everybody had to add their own little addition.

Every single body that my mom heard on that cassette she called their mothers up, and all the mothers listened to how talented we were with the rap game. Then our parents showed us equal talent in the spank game, because every single one of us got sent on so we could get beat on by our parents, as if our parents were going to share notes on who beat their child best for being the rap lyrical geniuses we were. I'm going to assume my mother was the king, because we used to call her the Muhammad Ali of ass whooping. My mom could handle you quick. My mom was so good at it.

CHAPTER THREE

My mom sent me to school on my tenth birthday. I had never had a birthday celebrated. I think none of us had. My siblings can only remember one birthday celebrated. My mother would pick a birthday that she would see as a hallmark birthday and celebrate that one, because you didn't get any other ones celebrated before that one. So my tenth birthday was my hallmark birthday and I got a cake. I got this beautiful pink-and-white striped shirt with this white sash over it, and my mother and my Aunt Senadia, who was a frequent guest in our home, was there and they came up with what they thought was the ultimate birthday gift for a ten-year-old girl coming of age. So my aunt and mother went to the store together and purchased me a mop, a broom, a dust pan, a mop bucket, Pine Sol, Clorox Bleach, SOS Pads, Comet, Ajax, and Brillo Pads and a couple of scouring pads, and a box of Tide laundry detergent and a box of bags so that I could load up the laundry and go to the laundry. That was my tenth birthday gift. And all because they thought it was so hilarious to give me cleaning supplies and call me "young lady" and tell me that it was my turn to take over the cleaning of the house and whatnot.

Of course it did happen. That's when I had to take over the cleaning of the house, but I remember being so furious that I think I hated everybody in the room, but I had to pretend I didn't so I could eat my cake. I couldn't be mad for my birthday. Somehow or another my mom and I got into an altercation, and I'm sure it was because of the tasteless gift she had purchased for me, and not just the fact that she had bought me this tasteless gift, but the fact that her and my entire family got to laugh at me. They took pictures of me in the bathroom, coming in and out of the bathroom crying, and I hated my family. I think I hated every single one at that moment, including my mother. I think I just hated my circumstances. I'm sure I didn't hate my family, but I thought that they were callous. They were callous to think that that was an appropriate gift for a ten-year-old girl who had never had a birthday party. It was callous for them to think that I would forget about it, because I didn't and I haven't. I'm forty-three years old, and obviously I haven't gotten over it.

The following morning, my mom and I continued this argument about my gift. Somehow or another she ended up slapping me across the face. I was wearing my brand new blouse, and I go to school with a bloody lip and nose because I wanted to teach her a lesson. I wanted to go to school with a bloody lip so the teachers could see just how she treated me at home. I quickly found out that once the teacher started investigating and asking me what had happened and why I was bleeding, I couldn't put it on my mother. I had to put it on the first person I could think of, which was my poor brother Jose, and I just said, "No, my brother Jose and I got into a fight before I came to school and I wanted to teach him a lesson so I didn't clean up."

My brother Jose had no clue what had happened, because he had already taken off to school when he saw that my mother and I were arguing. He took off ahead of me. He made it to Jefferson School before I did. When they pulled him out of class and questioned him about my bloody lip, he had no clue what I was talking about, but I remembered frowning and telling him to shut up and just go with it. He just accepted punishment for giving me a bloody lip when he knew he didn't give it to me. He knew it was my mom, and we were so afraid we were going to get taken from her by the CPS people, by the welfare folks, by the school folks. We didn't even know what folks. We thought the white folks were going to take us. We didn't know any better because we had been brought up to be afraid. We just thought they were going to up and take us. Grab us up and leave us, so we were taught to just not say anything.

Referring back to an incident when I was only about seven years old, I befriended this neighbor when we lived on Third Street. We became friends just because she was that white lady that was really nice and talked to me all the time. She would teach me words like "Hello." "Hello, Teresa. How are you doing?" Just basic words. I felt that she was my friend. I always thought that she was my friend. And one of those times I was headed to school she had asked if I'd seen a set of keys out in the yard.

I replied, "No, I did not. Why?"

She said, "I lost my keys in the front yard, and if you find them I will give you a dollar."

A dollar back when was a lot of money. I thought, *Man I'm going to spend this dollar. I'm going to buy a bag of chips. I'm going to buy a Whatchamacallit. I'm going to buy a KitKat and I'm going to buy a Wrigley's Chew.*

I had already spent my money in my mind, so I had no choice but to go find the keys so that I could literally spend my money on the things I wanted. The next day after I came home from school I spent what felt like hours, it was probably just minutes, looking around her car, around her front yard, up her stairs, down her stairs, back around her car, until as luck would have it God himself threw the keys underneath the wheel of her car. She had this station wagon-type car, and the keys were underneath her tire. I just couldn't believe it. I had gone and found the keys that were going to give me a dollar. They were going to get me to my candy and my soft drink quickly, also my chips. In my mind, I had bought the entire store with a dollar.

As I made my way up the stairs at her backdoor, it was open. I went in through the back stairs. Her back door was open, and I noticed that this black guy was yelling at her. I had never seen her with him but maybe I had once or twice but didn't really pay attention. This black guy was just yelling at her. I was just learning how to speak English, so I wasn't real sure. I caught every other word, but what I was able to make out of the yelling and screaming was that he was just out of jail and he was upset that she had been out and about doing some stuff she wasn't supposed to.

He was asking her about her whereabouts, what she had been doing, who she had been with, and she just kind of blew him off and told him leave her alone, she wasn't going to tell him anything. The more she blew him off, the angrier he got. I think he hit her a few times, but I wasn't real sure because I tried not to peek in. I was always taught to mind my own business and not get involved in the adult conversations. So a part of me said to run back home, come back and get your dollar tomorrow when she's done fighting with this guy. Another part of me looked at him and noticed that he was black, and I had heard through other people that, unfortunately, black men were bad and that they were mean sometimes and could do bad things they weren't supposed to. So I was preprogrammed to think he was bad because he was black, and I was preprogrammed to think that she was good because she was white. So, I kind of felt like somehow or another it was my obligation to see to it that she didn't get hurt somehow or another, because he was yelling at her and he was saying some awful things to her.

So I decided to just kind of stand there and look. Out of nowhere he just pulled something out of thin air or grabbed something. But, long story short, he grabbed a gun and just shot her in the neckline up against the fridge. When he shot her the first time, he actually pulled the trigger. It made me freeze. It reminded me of my dad. I froze. I tried to run. I told myself to run, but I was frozen. The more I told myself to run, the less I could run. So eventually I was able to run, turn back, and act as if I was running.

As I made it down the stairs, or at least a few of the stairs, I saw the guy at the top of the stairs looking at me. I was sure he was going to shoot me. I was convinced he was going to shoot me. I continued to walk down the stairs, or run down the stairs, but it felt like I was walking in mud. As soon as I made it to the bottom of the stairs, there was this tree right at the bottom of the stairs, so I thought about hiding in the back of the tree. As I went to hide in the back of the tree, I heard this *POW,* and this awful sound like a watermelon or something hollow hitting the stairs, and as I looked back, I noticed that he had shot himself and that his body had fallen backwards onto the stairs.

I ran across the street to tell my family, but by then the police had already been called because the neighbors had called them. He had shot the gal first, so when they heard the gunshot and the fighting, I'm assuming somebody called the police. By the time he shot himself, the police was already on their way. I ran across the street to go home to my grandmother's house, and my aunts came out and grandma came out. All the neighbors came out.

My family instructed me, "Don't say anything to the police." They asked me what I had seen, and I told them, but they said, "Don't talk to the police, because if you talk to the police, immigration is going to take your mom, and you guys are going to be taken back to Mexico."

They always scared us with stuff like that, and we didn't know any better. We never said anything. We just learned to shut up and mind our own business.

Back to me being ten years old, back to me being at the Race Track Tavern. We were taught not to tell on each other. So, even as my mom is questioning us on who did what, we knew better than to tell on one another. When the school was questioning me on who had hit me, I just instinctively knew to tell on my brother, because it was a lot easier for me to say my brother and I fought than it was to say that my mother had struck me in the face to where I bled. I learned to resent her, and I learned to love her at that same time, because when she would hit me I remember wishing harm upon her. I knew she picked apples in the apple fields.

They called my mom. They didn't believe that it was Jose. I don't believe that they believed it, because they called my mom and asked her about it. As soon as she walked into the room, I told my mom, "I'm sorry. Me and Jose got into a fight right before I came to school," and she kind of went along with it.

She said, "Why? Why did you guys fight like this?"

Like I said, we were preprogrammed to look out for each other. It wasn't right, but that's the way it was. My mother somehow or another knew that it was my responsibility as the oldest child to just step up to the plate and do what I was supposed to do, which was help her navigate her way through this thing. I was pretty smart early on, and I kind of caught on to things and was able to help her navigate. I felt that she could only do what she could do. The rest of it was up to my brothers and I to help her with.

We got along great. My brothers and I got along great. We fought a lot, but we got along great. Tight spaces will teach you how to love one another, teach you how to make up. Your mom spanking you teaches you to love her even after she spanked you, even if you don't like it at the time. Once it's said and done, we needed to be spanked. Sometimes even God has to spank us a little. We had to lose a little to know what we had.

What we had on Tenth Street was Race Track Tavern Days. We called it the Race Track Tavern Days because it was fun, fun, fun. So what we would do in the winter times, we would wet up the alley, because we knew that the drunks were coming out of the tavern. We knew about what time the drunks would be leaving the tavern, so we would wet up the alleyway with the hose or with buckets, because the hose would sometimes be turned off because of the winter. We would go inside the house and all of us fill up a bucket and then wet the street down a little bit. We used to wait until the drunks got onto the alley and wear our church shoes that were old and slippery on the bottom. We would wear our old church shoes and drag off the bumper as far as we could go. That was the goal, and we had the bumper Olympics.

It wasn't just us. It was us and the Gutierrezes, the Gudinezes, the Rodriguezes, and Elvis and his brothers. I can't think of their last name, but a bunch of our friends would get together with their old soccer cleats or church shoes, and I wore my old boots. We would strap them on, and we would precisely count to when the car would come into the alley, grab onto the bumper and hold on for dear life. He who held the longest was the champion. My brother Jose was usually the champion because he held on longest, also my brother Salvador, even some of our friends.

As you can tell, I guess I was a tomboy because, living on Tenth Street, we had a big walnut tree in the back of the house that we tied a gym rope onto, a big fat gym rope with a knot at the bottom. That was our playground. The big nut tree was our house. The rope was our way down, and that was our hangout spot. That's where we hung out all summer. We dug holes in the back and filled them up with the water hose and called it our own little pool. There were these old shacks right behind our house that had been abandoned for years and years. They were full of junk. We weren't allowed to go in there, so we were good about not going in there, but one day my brother Jose and, I think maybe, Salvador, were both on the rope at the same time.

We pushed them off the walnut tree onto the rope swing. They broke the rope swing and landed on the roof of one of the shacks. Jose landed on this homeless guy that had been sleeping there for I don't know how long. He had probably been sleeping there for a long time and we just didn't notice him, but there was this homeless drunk guy with the bluest of eyes, the whitest of skin, the whitest of hair, sleeping on one of the cabins. When my brother broke through the roof, he thought Satan was in there, so my brother was trying to break out of this place. He was trying to break out and he was screaming bloody murder. And then this white guy looks through the window and we were so scared. We started kicking down the door to get my brother out of the room because he was incarcerated with Satan. Jose peed his pants, but we promised not to tell on him. It was just the funniest thing ever.

After that little mishap, we broke one of the windows to get him out. Breaking the window gave us easy access to this place that was full of *Ebony* catalogues, old *Playboy* magazines—old, as in fifty years old or older. Also old Sears catalogues, a rocking chair, and a bunch of old stuff that had been left behind for years and years and years on end. That became probably my brothers' playing ground, because they had access to Sears catalogues and *Playboys*. So I'm sure that wasn't a very good thing for them to find. I never looked at the magazines, because I was a girl and I was preprogrammed not to, and I thought it was nasty, but I think my brothers might have. I'm pretty sure they probably did, and especially their friends. They should have held on to some of those *Playboys*, they would be worth something now, but they didn't.

Chapter Four

That was Tenth Street. Holding onto bumpers and watching drunk people fall coming from the tavern drunk. We used to call it the "Drunk Games." We used to sit out there with our friends and watch drunk people fall and hit the plaster, and we used to bet on who was going to hit the plaster first. We used to play dice out there with our friends. We used to play quarters. We used to play line. We used to play "drunk money, drunk horse." We just had a good time at that house.

Then we moved over to Fourth Street with my mother and then stepdad. We lived on Fourth Street for a few years. By then we had bikes and whatnot. I had this big, beautiful bike. It was a banana bike called the "Blue Dove." This powder-blue bike with this big, long, banana seat with clouds on the chain guard called "Blue Dove." I remember loving that bike so much that I was on it 24/7, with strings and cans hanging out from behind a skateboard. I used to tie my younger brother Jason's skateboard, a box, and a skateboard contraption. We used to put a milk crate on his skateboard with a string, and I used to ride my baby brother around there.

We used to put pillows and blankets in it because he was a baby. He was only eight or nine months old, and we loved him. He was our toy, and I used to put him back there and ride him up and down the street to comfort him and make him happy, to put him to sleep, and just enjoy hearing him giggle. We dropped him over a few times. We got in trouble for dropping him on the floor a few times, but either way he was all right. He loved it, we loved it. We had a great time with him.

At this stage we're on Fourth Street, and my stepdad is starting to drink heavy. Along with the drinking heavy, I think he started to do drugs, because his behavior was starting to change and my mom and him were starting to fight a lot. It reminded me a little bit of when my dad was alive. They used to get physical sometimes and put their hands on each other. Then he started being a nasty *chimo* and I ended up telling my mother on him. I told her what he was doing, and he told my mother, and swore on the Virgin Mary, that I was making it up and that he was not doing it. But he had been doing it. He just wouldn't own up to it.

I finally confronted him in front of my mother, where he eventually confessed that he was being nasty. But by then it didn't matter to me, because I felt like I didn't trust him or her. So it was just a matter of me taking care of myself. My mom and him started having more and more problems, and they split up. One of my uncles gave my mother the suggestion to go to the coast to Skagit Valley to go pick berries and make money for the summer so she could get ahead, and if she took all of us with her she would really get ahead, because she would have at least three or four kids that could pick as well as she could.

So we went to the coast to Burlington, Washington, and we picked berries. I met a girl by the name of Sedalia, and she became my best friend real quickly. We were about the same age. She was a few years older than I was, but she quickly became my friend. I went to night school with my cousins, Carmen and Anna Alvarez, because they went to night school. They were taking ESL. I didn't need ESL, but I figured my mom yanked me out of school early, so why not get some credits and why not go do something other than work in the fields? Go to school. So I went to Burlington Middle

School with my cousins, and we would all ride to school together and come back home together. There was a bus that actually picked us up at the Sakuma Camps if you wanted to go to night school, which was kind of cool.

So we went to school, and one day when I'm at school in mid-July, it was after the Fourth of July, I don't remember the exact date, but mid-July, my friend Sedalia shows up in my class. I'm actually asked to go to the office. When I go to the office, I see my friend Sedalia waiting at the office for me, and she gives me a couple of signs to tell me to "Shhh" and not say much. Well, what they told me was that they made up a note saying that my uncle had been involved in an awful auto accident and then they needed to take me back home. What was really going on is that Sedalia wanted me to hang out with her and skip school and go have some burgers and go back home. I am assuming this because me and her had not talked about me skipping or me hanging out with her or me going anywhere with her, but when she showed up it seemed like a good idea. It seemed like, "Well, they went through the trouble of getting me out of school. Why not? Let's go to McDonald's and have a burger or whatnot." But I didn't read too much into it until her brother, who liked me, and I guess in fairness I thought he was cute too, had been talking to his brother-in-law, who had been picking on him about if he liked a girl enough he should take her.

So him and his brother-in-law had been taunting each other about him taking me. As a matter of fact, his brother-in-law, Reyes, and his brother Juan bet him fifty bucks that he wouldn't just take me. I think he felt pressured, because his brother-in-law probably taunted him to some degree. He felt pressured to follow through and take me, to show his brother-in-law he was a real man of sorts and took it upon himself to take his sister to school, bring in a note to take me from school, and then tell me that I'm being taken. At first I guess I thought it was sort of funny. Like, "Yeah right! Taken? How? Why?" And then I thought, *Nah, he's not going to take me, because he's taking her. Why is he going to take two people?*

Then we went to McDonald's and the brother-in-law showed up. I don't even know if he was taunting him or just playing with him—like, no man don't do it or whatnot, which taunted him even more, and he just had it in his mind that he was going to take me to Texas, and that's what it was. He was going to take me to Texas. Well, meanwhile, after he's taking me to Wapato first before he takes me to Texas, because he has a sister that lives in Wapato, his mother comes over to talk to my mother and tell my mother that her son had taken me from school. Not to worry about me, not to call the authorities, that I was in no harm's way, that her son had just taken me as his bride. I'm not sure what my mom had to be thinking, but she didn't even call the authorities. So the way I figure it is that I was tainted goods because I was in the possession of a man, and all I would have done is brought shame onto my family. So I guess I was predestined to stay there.

So he took me quickly to work in the fields to pick cucumbers in Woodburn, Oregon, where we spent a few months picking cucumbers. Two weeks into him taking me, I realized that this was not for me and I had to get away from him, and followed by the fact that he was showing his abusive side and I was scared of him. One of the days that we were out picking cucumbers, his brother and him got into an altercation about speed, or how slow I was or how fast I was, and something about my grandma, the champion. I was a child, so I had nothing to talk about but my family and my grandmother, and I kept telling them and insisting to them that my grandmother was a good field worker, which eventually made to where I should have been a good hard worker myself, which eventually led to me getting in trouble because I wasn't as fast as I could be.

Two weeks into me being taken, I get a moment where I can run off and get away, and I take my chance and I run. I run through the corn. Well, first I didn't just run through the field. I asked to go to the bathroom, and that would give me enough time so he wouldn't worry about where I was at and not working. I asked to go to the bathroom, and when he wasn't paying attention I ran into the cornfield, and just kept running through the cornfield until I found a place, a little house in the middle of the corn field, some farmer's house. I knocked at the door and asked them to please let me in, and I quickly explained to them that I had been taken from my home and that the man that took me was out in the fields.

So these people decide to go ahead and let me in their house and hide me from him. When he's hiding me, the gentleman decides I should stay away from the door and away from where I can be seen, and his wife and him stay in the living room. Then we hear the knocking on the door, but when we hear the knocking on the door the gentleman knows just by looking at me that he has to send me back out, because the guy on the other side of the door was very unhappy that they had allowed me in and that they were going to cover for me or hide me or send me back to the authorities, or whatever was running through his mind. He was just not going to let them even call the police. So he quickly knocked on the door and told them that if they didn't throw me out he would kick the door down and kill both of them and still take me. So it was in their best interest to just let me out, which they did.

So I went back to work, got in trouble for trying to run off, accepted my whooping that I had coming, and decided I wouldn't run off quite yet. Then I was taken to California to live in this town called Button Willow, where I eventually got pregnant. So here I am, thirteen years old, living in Button Willow, California, pregnant but unable to go to the doctor because I'm a baby.

So we live in Button Willow until I'm starting to show, which is about four months. Friends of my sister-in-law come over to dinner. Well, they don't come over to dinner. They come over to invite us to dinner. They came over as company and then invited us to dinner. When they invited him and I to go to dinner with them and I replied no because I have nothing to wear and I'm kind of fat and I have nothing to wear, I guess I learned that I couldn't just say anything, because anything I said was going to be condemning. The minute I said that to those people, he quickly got real silent, real pale white, and said to them that he wasn't interested in going to dinner with them and neither was I. Thank you very much for the offer, but have a good day, and asked me to go to the room with him.

As soon as I went to the room with him, he told me, "As soon as people leave I'm going to beat your ass for announcing to those people that you're pregnant with a piece of shit that can't even buy you maternity clothes. You're just trying to embarrass me. You're trying to knock on my manhood, and I'm going to teach you what women need to be taught when they knock on men's manhood."

I don't have to go in to detail to what took place next. By the time my sister-in-law came back home, he had already pretty much beaten me to submission to where I would never talk about him not buying me the proper clothing. Quickly after that, about a month after that, we came back to the state of Washington because asparagus season was about to start and we needed to come back and pick asparagus.

So we moved back to Toppenish, Washington. Actually no, we moved back to Wapato, Washington, in his sister's house and picked asparagus. I got to pick asparagus until my seventh or eighth month of pregnancy with my son, and I would get a bunch of nosebleeds because we were out in the sun all day long without water, without food, without proper toilets. We had outhouses that we could go use. But other than that, the food that we ate was food that I had packed that morning that sat in the windshield throughout the day until we were able to eat. And because we were bending down all day to pick the asparagus, you couldn't eat a lot of food because you would just throw it right back up.

So here I am, thirteen years old, pregnant as all get out, ready to have my firstborn child, and no proper nutrition, no proper prenatal care, and a high-risk pregnancy. And then, to just make things worse, my child is breech, but we don't know this until it's time to go give birth. After being in labor for twelve hours at home, I finally get to make it to the hospital, because things are not looking good, and a doctor in Toppenish, Washington, has to extract my child because he is coming in full fetal. The doctor leaves a gauze inside my uterus after the cesarean. Nine days into it I have something called toxic shock, septic shock, and everything that comes along with it. I had a heart attack, which left me with a stint.

I spent six weeks on life support in three different hospitals. Nobody had a clue what was going on, until one doctor in the main hospital went back and looked for the gauze and did a re-caesarian, opened up my stomach, found the gauze, and cleaned out my guts, because my guts were full of pus and infection. The doctor that left the gauze inside me didn't have the common courtesy to pull it out, so a specialist ended up removing the cotton that the first doctor had left inside me, but not until after I was sick with toxic shock syndrome as any human person can be.

Six weeks in the hospital, finally get out for the holidays, but because I was in the hospital for so long I became paralyzed from the waist down. I had to learn how to walk again. So I had to go to therapy and learn how to walk again. This is all of December into January. February comes along. My brother-in-law decides to get married for Valentine's, so I'm taken back to Mexico with my then newborn son to be a part of a wedding that I don't get to even dance at because I was so sick. I couldn't participate in the fiesta part, so my captor's family was nice enough to bring him a young fifteen-year-old girl he could dance with, because he needed somebody he could enjoy the evening with and because I was fresh out of the hospital. I could not do it, so that was probably the first and only time I've ever felt jealousy in my life, because I felt jealousy to watch this man, no matter how evil how horrible he was, I felt jealousy watching him dance with another female. I don't know why, nor am I interested in trying to figure out why, but it is the one time I have felt jealousy, and it's the last time, because thank God that's a button I was able to turn off. I don't have a jealous bone in me. So thank God for that. Thank God for a lot of the bad things that happened, because they have helped me help myself along the way.

Here I am in Mexico. How they didn't nab him at the border bringing me back is beyond me. Another oversight by INS. Why didn't the doctor didn't CPS while I was on life support when I'm a fourteen-year-old girl who just had a child and who is spending this much time in the hospital? Why nobody bothered to call anybody to come and help. I later confronted the doctor months later. I'm not exactly sure how much later. I went to the doctor's office and I asked him why didn't he call CPS, why didn't he fend for me. His exact answer was it was my fault, because my people were well known for having unprotected sex young, and my people are well known for wanting to be married as husbands and wives early on in life, and that was not his fault. It was my people's fault. So I didn't know what to do or say to that. I just figured sum it up to okay and went on my merry way.

Years later I contacted an attorney who is now governor, but then was just a small attorney in Selah, Washington. I hired him to represent me on this malpractice case. He told me what I guess is normal practice for young attorneys, but what he told me was that he could not represent me on a lawsuit, even though I had a good lawsuit, because he couldn't find doctors that would testify against a local doctor, because he was a local hero and that people in little towns like Yakima, Washington, and Toppenish, Washington, and Wapato, Washington, don't turn their backs on each other. So the chances of me finding a doctor that would testify against the doctor that left the gauze were slim pickings. So he basically told me to brush it off and be thankful that I was alive, and that there was nothing he could do for me. Again, this man holds a very powerful position in our state now, which is ironic. Now it makes absolute sense why he didn't represent me. He needed the votes for the future, and he needed the doctors and the lawyers and the friends of friends to put him in the position he was in now.

I was just an insignificant little Mexican, so it was not worth him throwing his career away for somebody like me. So I suppose to some great sense of satisfaction he did what he had to do for himself, and I'm still here, so I guess I didn't need a favor. So I never pursued a lawsuit against the doctor after I was told no. I figure I chalked it up to I'm just glad I'm alive and I'm glad I'm here. I had no clue that that toxic shock syndrome would follow me to this day, that I would be suffering and dying of autoimmune disorder, rheumatoid arthritis, COPD, pituitary disorder, gallbladder disorder, pancreatitis, and the last one is gastroparesis, paralysis of my insides. I'm forty-three years old, and I guess I'm facing shutdown.

CHAPTER FIVE

We're back to the state of Washington. Now it's about April. The asparagus season has started, and I have to figure out how I'm going to go pick asparagus when I just got out of rehab months earlier. Nobody was there to tell me I shouldn't have just gone back to the fields. Nobody was there to tell him that he shouldn't take me back to the fields. Even if they had I don't think he would have listened. He would still have taken me to the fields, because that's what he knew. That was his natural environment. All the women around him worked in the fields. His mother worked in the fields. So if the fields were good enough for his mother and his sisters, I guess the fields were certainly good enough for me.

We're back into the fields. This is April, and I'm taking my son with me because we usually work at dark. Asparagus is best picked from 2:30 in the morning, get out of the fields by 9:00. We try to be out of there by 10:00, because if you're not then it's too hot. It's too hard on your back. It's too hard on your kidneys, because your kidneys are facing the sun the entire day and there's no drinking water. The farmers won't, or can't, have drinking water out there for you. We're just happy to have outhouses to go to the toilet. Here I am in the fields with a man that is actually really good at what he does. So he can outrun me and he can outwork me, but this is what he has been doing. Thus, he expects me to work as fast as he does, and I'm in trouble many times because I can't keep up. Not just that I just get out of the hospital, not just that I just learned how to walk again, but I also have a child that's requiring me to breast feed him when he wakes up.

So my ear has to be to the wind listening for my crying child in the backseat of a car and also focused on keeping up with this professional asparagus picker. There were many times that he went out drinking and couldn't, or wouldn't, pick in the morning. He would drive me to work when he's still drunk, with a child in the backseat, gets me to the fields, jumps in the backseat, puts my child in the front seat, and tells me to get out there and pick. It's not like I can say no. It's not like I have a choice. So I have to get out there and pick wearing nothing but a headlamp because it is dark out. The only way you can pick in the dark is with a headlamp attached to your forehead.

So here I am working in the pitch dark, angry, scared, frustrated and not feeling well. But it's not like I really have a choice, so I have to push along and do what I have to do to not get beat down. Then somewhere in the dark this horrible, horrible, horrible image scared every little bit of life I had in me, because when I lifted my head I noticed a set of eyes looking back at me in the dark. All I could think of was the devil. All I could think of was a ghost. All I could think of was … I don't even know what I was supposed to think of; I just know that I was scared for my life. So I put my head back down and started to pray to God. I felt that if I pray to God enough and closed my eyes tight enough, God would take care of it. I put my head up again and noticed that the eyes were still staring at me. I knew I had no choice but to deal with it.

So I started to point my knife at this figure and started praying at it and swooshing it away and whistling off and trying to kick some dirt around to try to get it to go away. This thing wouldn't move. This thing just stared at me. I could hear it breathe. The more I heard it breathe, the more scared I was, the more I prayed.

Eventually it went away, and I thought I had prayed it away.

A few hours later I look up into the distance and there comes this big, wild-looking dog coming my way, and again I was scared. I didn't know what to think of it. Earlier on it had taunted me, but it didn't really do anything. It didn't growl. It didn't do anything but breathe. Then it took off and it came back, so now I must deal with it. So I poked the knife at it and I asked it to leave and threw little pieces of rock at it, not rock but dirt, dry dirt, hard dirt. We call them *terramotos*, which is dry, wet dirt. I tried flinging a few at it and see if it would take off, and instead of taking off it came closer to me and tried to be my friend.

It turns out it was this big pit bull that ran off from its owners or wandered off or was probably thrown out in the middle of a field by, I'm assuming, bad owners. It friended me and became my companion throughout the day, and I even shared my lunch with this dog who would go home with me at the end of the day. I couldn't find it in me to leave it behind. Even though I wasn't much of a dog owner and never had a dog, I figured the dog found me, and I took it as a sign and it was up to me to be nice to the dog.

So I took the dog home and fed him leftovers. I never bought it dog food, because the way I figured he followed me home, he was going to eat what I eat. So table scraps is what it was, and the dog stayed my dog for a long time, for many years. One day he just ran off or died or something. I'm not sure what happened to it. I don't remember, but I just know that he was my dog for a few years. Looking back at it now, I'm sure it was God that sent me that dog to keep an eye on me and help me out in the darkness so I wouldn't be so afraid of the dog.

Like I said, I finished off the asparaguses and went into the rest of the harvest. By now my son is starting to walk and starting to get himself in some trouble. We live in this trailer park, Willow Tree, in Toppenish, Washington, and I meet what's going to become my very close friend and my daughter's godmother. We weren't allowed to be friends initially. So we had to be secret friends, because my brother-in-law insisted that there was something wrong with me being friends with the white lady next door, that she would teach me things that I did not need to know. She would Americanize me or Westernize me too soon, where I would want to treat my husband like an equal, and that was not my place. My place was not ever to treat him equal, but for him to be boss and me not to be.

Either way, I didn't care. She was a good gal that I met, and she cooked well and kept a beautiful home, and I felt that going to her house sometimes got me away from my madness, from my crazy life, from my oddball circumstance. Her life seemed to be what I felt was a normal life. She was married. They had one child. At the time they didn't have a child, but they were headed towards one child, and she liked hanging out with me so much so that she would wash her clothes by hand, even though she had a washer and dryer that worked perfectly well. I wasn't allowed to have a washer and dryer, because I was told that those modern gadgets make women lazier because we forget how to do things without power and without modern conveniences. So I guess I was stuck with the washboard and a washtub to hand wash our field clothes, which were soaked in mud and dried dirt and dried stains and sometimes blood if we cut ourselves at work. Nor here nor there, hand washing was all right at the time.

So I had to hand wash my baby's clothes too, and I felt like I was always handwashing, but I had to do what I had to do. My *comadre* looks back and tells me that she thought it was so funny that my son, Jesse, would straddle his crib like a horse and he rode his crib to the floor. That was probably the first time she entered my house. I was embarrassed to have her come inside my house, because I felt that her house was so much prettier than mine. I kept a clean house. I just kept a simple, poor, clean house, and I was really good at making things, doilies and baby clothes and pillow cases. I was a bit of a crafty gal, and that was one of the things that he enjoyed or liked that I did, and so did his family. It made me look like a woman, or made me feel like I was part of the women's circle. So I had to do what I had to do to keep up with them, and stitching was the way I did that. Cooking was an important thing in their family too.

But my comadre and I hung out together enough that I guess she reminded me that that was not my life. I was not to live in a trailer park in a $500 trailer for my entire life. I made the best of it. I eventually stopped working in the fields and just had a little store out of my trailer so that the father of my kids could go out and work. I stayed running the store, because I was obviously not going to be very good at continuing in the fields. He kind of picked up that I was a little bit smarter than the average Joe.

So I ran a store from house. I cooked food and sold burritos my father-in-law had taught me to make. Actually, my father-in-law was very nice to me. He loved me like a daughter, I believe. He always told me that he loved me the most, that out of his daughters-in-law that I was his favorite, and out of many people that knew I was his favorite person. He enjoyed talking to me, and he enjoyed asking me to find things that he hadn't found for a long time. Sometimes he would just tell me out of the blue, "Have you seen my old hammer?" And maybe I had a picture memory of some sort, but I always knew were things were at.

Like I said, maybe I had a photographic memory where I just remembered items in certain areas, and I would sometimes just say something to say it just to get a reaction from him. I would tell him go over to the washroom on top of the two-by-four to the right, to the left and it's in the corner, and my father-in-law would always go where I told him and find it. Sometimes it was just a coincidence, and sometimes I really did know that it was there. He would just laugh about it and we became close friends.

I quickly knew who I could be friends with in the family and who I had to be careful of, who I couldn't say too much around, because he had a sister that, if you said any little thing, would spread it like butter and make miracles out of it, and she would say the most asinine things that came to her mind. She was not a very good person. Then he had this other sister that I lived with for a while who is actually very nice. We lived together in Wapato, and when I was first pregnant we lived together in California. She was actually pretty nice. She became my close friend, and my sister-in-law and I knew there were certain things I just couldn't disclose to her, but there was a lot that we talked about, and there was a lot that she told me, and a lot that I learned from her.

Her children loved me. I was their age, but they called me aunt. They still do, but ironically I was about their age. I loved them. So if they had a dirty diaper, I would change it. If they had a dirty nose, I would blow it. If they were hungry, I would feed them, because I saw them as I saw my family, part of my circle. I loved them and still do. My nieces and nephews always responded very well to me too. I think I was that cool young aunt. They thought I was pretty and that I was just cool, because I knew modern music and I would turn up my radio where nobody else did and I would sing and dance with them. I would sing off-key.

I guess it wasn't all bad. I grew up with my nieces and nephews as if they were my siblings. I learned that my sister-in-law's job was to teach me how to be an adult, but ultimately they were his sisters, and anything I said bad about him would get back to him. So it was best if I keep to myself about my feelings and my emotions, and even about the abuse. I was only given permission to vent for a little while, and then I had to put my feelings away and not deal with it anymore. Get over having a black eye and learn how to cover it up and keep on marching.

My comadre, however, would tell me, "You're not supposed to put up with that. You know that. He's not supposed to treat you that way." But she never got involved. She would always just tell me that it was not right the way I lived, and that if I ever needed to get out that there was people and organizations that were out there that could help me, and maybe she planted the seed that would eventually lead to me leaving and staying out. I don't know now, and I probably didn't know then, but like I said, a lot of people had a lot to do with my being here, my being who I am and my being exactly how I am, good or bad.

I eventually talk him into going back to Yakima. I don't know why I felt Yakima was better for me, but I think that deep down inside I always felt like Yakima was where my mom would someday come back to and I would get to see her, or that Yakima was where my family lived, even though I didn't visit them or they didn't visit me. I just wanted to be closer to them somehow. I moved into this place on Pleasant Avenue, across the street from a school, with my young son. I had a neighbor who was a truck driver. She and her husband were both truck drivers. Her name was Vera. I can't think of his name, but they had a daughter, and their daughter became friends with my son. I became friends with their daughter, and their daughter and I would walk across the street to the middle school and play tennis.

So I felt like playing tennis with her helped me secretly play like a child with a child without feeling responsible, because I wasn't doing some adult activity like cooking or cleaning or sewing or parenting or something like that. I always felt that when I hung out with their child, my twelve-year-old child was playing with their twelve-year-old child, and I was able to get away from my tornado of emotions that I was trying to suppress. Vera became my friend quickly, but she knew we couldn't really visit with each other a lot, but she knew she was my friend. She collected every McDonald's toy in the world. I think her child was into collecting McDonald's toys, and when I went over to her place it also felt like a very comfortable place to be at, because they had one child, a fish tank, and a whole bunch of McDonald's toys throughout their house. Maybe the McDonald's toys made me feel comfortable, or maybe just the fact that Vera was a big, tough woman that I knew could kick some ass.

Ironically, she would fend for me a few times. When she could tell that he was hitting on me she would pound the wall and yell through the wall, tell him to stop, tell him to pick on somebody his own size, tell him to pick on a man. One day she surprised the hell out him when she came whipping through the door with a baseball bat and started beating the hell out of him because he was beating the hell out of me.

I remember she told me, "Run to my house, child. This is the last time this idiot hits you." And she started thomping on him, and told him that if he came over next door to take me, that she would see to it that she would break his face in half with a baseball bat and call the cops on him.

So she kept him away from me for a few days. Of course, a few days later I was a little too afraid and maybe just didn't want to inconvenience her by sticking around. I eventually went home and accepted my punishment for staying at Vera's overnight. I'm thankful to her. She made me understand that women could kick butt too and that it was all right to defend yourself.

A few months after that, we're both in the apartment talking about something that eventually results in an argument that eventually results in him hitting me. As I'm laying on the floor looking up at him, and he is crouched over me and continuously slapping me, out of nowhere it was like God himself put the tennis racket within arm's reach. I found the tennis racket, and he wasn't paying attention to what I was doing because he was too busy hitting me, when out of nowhere I just hit him with the tennis racket across the head and just started pouncing on him. He looked like a waffle after I was done.

As a matter of fact, my brother Sal bumped into him about a week later, and he couldn't help but laugh and said, "What happened to your face, man? You look like Leggo my Eggo." I don't even know why it's funny. Maybe because it gave a great deal of satisfaction to kick his ass for once, and it gave me a great deal of satisfaction to give him a couple of really good ones that would stick with him, because he knew what it felt like to lick your own wounds and have bruises that you had to deal with and couldn't talk to anybody about.

However, after the John McEnroe moment—because that's what I felt like, I felt like John McEnroe, I felt like I John McEnroed him—I started hitting him back from that moment forward. I couldn't really defend myself, so I don't know why I even tried. He was so much stronger than I was, and so much meaner than I was, but I still tried sticking up for myself as many times as I could.

Sometimes he would do sheer stupid things. This one particular time, he convinced me to go fishing with him at a lake in Buena, and it was a hot, hot summer day, so I went. We took our child, and he invited a couple other family members to go with us. I don't know how we went from fishing off the dock to him thinking it was funny to push me into the pond, into Buena Lake. When he pushes me into this pond, I didn't know how to swim and he knew it, but he just thought it was hilarious. He thought it was hilarious to watch me splash and fight for my life, and I would imagine drinking nasty pond water, to the point where just out of nowhere my fight was gone. I must have been drowning, and I vaguely remember touching the bottom of the lake and the plants around the lake. I don't even know what it's called, but that green stuff that wraps around your legs.

Out of nowhere, somebody else jumps into the lake, grabs me by my hair, pulls me out, and allows me to throw up. I would imagine he gave me CPR, and after throwing up I realized that it wasn't even him who threw me in the lake. It was a random stranger that happened to be at the lake that jumped in after me. He thought it was ridiculous that everybody else stood around and watched me drown, and they were too afraid to confront this idiot, because even though he was their brother, he was very aggressive, and everybody was afraid of him because he was kind of like a pit bull.

You never knew when he would strike. He argued with everybody, including his father. Everybody was afraid of him. He was so much bigger and stronger than any one of them that everybody, minus probably one of his brothers, was afraid of him. I think he just thought it was funny. They didn't know how to react, or they might have thought it was funny too. I don't know. To this day I'm afraid of swimming and I'm afraid of lakes. It's not the lake's fault, and it's not the pond's fault. It's my fault for not learning how to swim. I guess nor here nor there on that.

I become pregnant with my second child and I'm in my second trimester. By then we had a falling out with one of his family members—actually a few, but one mainly. We went to visit his family back at the trailer park, and I'm pregnant with child number two, when one of my sisters and I were just talking and out of nowhere I just felt this amazing weight land on me, but I wasn't expecting what was taking place. One of his sisters assaulted me while I was sitting on a bucket, and I guess I didn't pay attention that she was coming my direction, and she just assaulted me, and I'm not sure that she knew that I was pregnant. I believe she did, but I don't know now, and I've since become her friend again and we've since patched this up. So I've never asked if she knew I was pregnant, if she knew she killed my child when I was in my second trimester.

I don't even think about that child, and I don't even talk about that child. I don't know why. I haven't thought about this child for twenty-some years. I guess I never thought of it as a child because it never happened, because I never gave birth to it, because I never had a caesarian, because I lost it, because the child died. It was easier not to think of the child, to think of the great pain I felt to lose a child in the second trimester when your stomach was already showing.

All I have left is a memory of one picture of me pregnant with the child that died. I rarely look at it because I don't want to think about it, because if I think about it I have to deal with it. I don't think about it. I can keep it packed up away as a child that died or a miscarriage, God's not wanting me to have one child I can't take care of in the future, I guess.. So it's easier to just put it away.

CHAPTER SIX

After my child died, I wouldn't meet my friends for about six months. We moved out of Pleasant and moved back to Fourth Street, ironically to the place I lived at before I was taken. I don't know how I mixed up my places of living, but thinking about this unborn child, I guess it mixed the dates in head and my dates were off.

When we moved back to Fourth Street, I'm pregnant with my third child, my now middle child, my daughter. We were happy. For a split second in time he was wonderful, and I was happy to be his wife, and I was happy to be carrying twins, and he was happy to be the father of twins. So he was different during this pregnancy than he had been with the first two. He was happy to be having this baby. He was happy to buy me maternity clothes. He was happy to buy me whatever I was craving. He was happy to make me happy. I saw a side of him that nobody had seen, and that was the side of the guy who was happy to have … The funny part is, he wasn't just happy to be my daughter's father, but he was happy to be both my girls' father, Anabel and Abigail. Abigail never made it, because halfway through my pregnancy the second child stopped developing, and the second child, because it was in her own bag, was able to spare Anabel's life, and he was just happy to have a daughter. At this stage it didn't matter that he had lost a daughter. He was just happy that we had saved one.

From our experience with the prior two pregnancies, he knew that being in my second trimester didn't necessarily mean that I was out of the blue. It just meant that I was in my second trimester. It think that he learned from our first experience with losing a child and then now being pregnant and losing a second child. I think somehow he understood that I wasn't healthy, and in order for me to have a healthy birth he needed to cut me some slack, which he did. This time around the pregnancy was much different than the first two. This time around he is more cavalier about it. He's more grown up about it. He's a lot more excited. It's as if we were having our first child for the first time. I think at this point I made a decision to stick it out with him, stay with him, be his wife, be the mother of his children, and I felt like there was a lot of room for growth, not only in him but in the both of us.

I understood that some of his ways were implemented by his parents. He had learned what he had learned from his parents. He had learned field work from his parents. They were migrants and they followed the crops, so he only knew what he knew. I still wasn't able to figure out why he was so mean and so aggressive, and why he drank so much and why he did so many drugs. I wouldn't figure this out for another few years down the road. All I knew right now was my comadre and her husband became very close friends, and he learned something from our comadre. He learned that there was another way other than just the fields.

Her and her husband at the time were selling Amway. So they were very mixed into this Amway positive way of thinking and positive projecting of their life and their success and where they saw themselves a year from now, ten years from now, a hundred years from now, and I think some of that positivity that Amway had taught them was rubbing off on us. They were certainly sparking a dream in me, because they were showing me that there was great success out there to be had. They were showing him that there was something else other than working in the fields, which helped him cut me some slack. I wasn't forced to work in the fields when I was pregnant with my twin girls. It went to go work for the school district. I went to work with a gal named Lori Sevenie. She was a kindergarten teacher and I was her assistant. I was her TA.

While I'm her TA, I'm pregnant with my girls. I start working on my dream, and he starts allowing me to work partially on my dream, because he felt me working in an elementary school was a safe zone. There weren't any guys around me. It was just children and teachers and safe people. So he started giving a little. I started giving a little, and he started looking forward to my paycheck. I had a steady check, whereas migrant workers did not. You only had a check when there were crops, and when there were no crops there was no money. So he started leaning to my way of thinking and allowing me to kind of better myself to some degree, but with his consent and his permission and his micromanaging my actual success. I was only allowed to do so much and then I was capped off.

I was only allowed to be a TA. I couldn't go back to college and become a full-fledged teacher, because then I would learn things in college that would tell me to leave him, and he wasn't comfortable with that. So the way I figured is that if he let me work for the school district, and not have me working in the fields, I was better served than trying to combat him and go right back to the fields where I didn't want to be. So I figured he gave a little, I had to give a little.

Eventually I went from working at the school district to working for the State of Washington for the Department of Disabilities, for DDD, a place called Selah School. When I went to work for Selah School I started bringing in good money monthly, guaranteed, day in, day out. I was then stuck doing a lot of overtime, because when he had no work I was the primary breadwinner. There were many times I was the primary breadwinner and he had no job. I had to take care of the four of us. I took care of him, myself, and my two children. He started seeing that I was able to make more money. He was able to work less, drink more, do more drugs, and not have to be responsible for showing up for work the next day, because I carried the load. I realized that that was not going to work for me. I'm not going to be the primary breadwinner, caregiver, and supplier of all. The more he drank, the more irresponsible he became, the more responsible I had to become, the more accountable and the more focused my dreams became. I knew it was a matter of time before I outgrew him, before I educated myself enough to support myself.

He wasn't paying attention to the big picture. I was. He was just micromanaging me to some degree, but he was so focused on his own problems that he wasn't paying attention to my growth.

Funny story: before I actually went to go work for the State of Washington, so some time between when I was working at the school district to when I worked for the State of Washington, I went and did a JTPA (on-the-job training program) for Yakima Valley Farm Workers Clinic. When I worked at clinic I was able to meet doctors that spoke Spanish, and in meeting these doctors that spoke Spanish, I realized that people that spoke Spanish could go to medical school, that people that spoke Spanish went off to graduate school and became great doctors, and even the ones that were not doctors, there were nurses, and even the ones that were not nurses were receptionists.

There was this one gal there that spoke both English and Spanish, and her job was to talk to the Mexican moms about not having so many children. Talk to them about birth control. Talk to them about not being victims of abuse. Talk to them about sticking up for themselves. Talk to them about, even though you left Mexico, Mexico has to leave you. At some stage you have to catch on to the Western way of doing things, which is you don't allow a man to hit you. If you earn an income, it's yours. You can utilize it. You're also 50 percent of the big picture, not 20 percent, 30 percent, but 50 percent. You're an equal partner to your partner.

The more I listened, even though I wasn't being talked to directly,

I was paying attention and I was growing. Ester was, at this point, my new role model. I've looked up to a lot of strong women and some strong men, but mainly some strong women, in my life, and I went back to that second-grade teacher that I looked up to, Ms. Vevins. I looked up to her more than anybody else probably in my life. Looking at Ester, I thought, *Wow, she's also got the American dream. She is a Mexican gal married to a white man who has bettered herself, who has taken strides over anybody else that I know that is of Mexican descent.* I clung on to that and I shadowed her, even though she didn't know. She knows now because I've since talked to her, but I shadowed her and I looked at the way she carried herself. Her hair was always perfectly done. Her makeup was perfectly done. She always had long, beautiful nails, and she walked with this sense of urgency. She walked fast, and wherever she was going she walked fast and sexy, and this lady was a full-busted, older lady that was full of charisma and beauty. She was very elegant.

I wanted to do nothing more than to be just like her. One day she came up to me and pulled me aside and said, "Teresa, can I talk to you about a sensitive issue?"

I was so afraid that she was going to talk to me about being an abuse victim and how I shouldn't tolerate it. I thought, *She's read me like an open book. She knows exactly what I'm going through and she's about to counsel me on abuse*, and I didn't know how to deal with that. I didn't know how I was supposed to respond to that. I had all the answers lined up in my head of the questions I thought she was going to ask me or the subject matter that she was going to talk to me about.

I went to the side with her and I was nervous. I asked her what she wanted to talk to me about. She said, "Are those your natural boobs?"

I said, "Yeah." It's the first time anybody had ever acknowledged my breasts.

She said, "You have beautiful breasts. You're a D, or at least a

DD, as far as I can see."

I said, "I don't even know what I am."

She goes, "I can tell. I can tell by the flimsy bra that you're wearing that doesn't fit you. The straps are falling to the side, and I can tell it's probably only one of the two bras that you own."

I thought, *Not only is she wise, but she is a mind reader and she is psychic. Has she been to my house?* She just looks at me and just smiles and takes this bag that she had set aside and grabs it and just gives it to me, hands it to me.

She said, "Here's a couple of pretty blouses that I believe will fit you pretty, and there's a couple bras that I thought you would enjoy. You're about my size, except you're smaller. You're a little twig, but you've got beautiful breasts. Enjoy those, because those will go away, and if you don't take care of them they'll sag. Yes, they'll sag."

I looked at her and I thought, *Wow, you were already my role model, but thank you. Thank you for the bras and thank you for the great advice. I get to wear your shirt. Wow! Okay, let's go home and put on one of these bras.* Funny that I would even think about that, because she influenced me to buy good bras. She actually influenced me to go to Nordstrom's and get measured properly for size and then go buy the bras at another store like a good shopper would. Start at Walmart and move my way up from there, but I didn't have Nordstrom's dollars.

So here I am working at the Farmers Clinic, paying attention to these strong women, paying attention to farm workers that were coming in complaining about stuff that I knew a lot about because I was just there with them.

I quickly graduated from the clinic to the State of Washington because of pay, but before I left there I have a funny story about the clinic. He came to pick me up at five o'clock, because that was the time I normally was released. What it didn't know was that the clinic closes at five. That doesn't mean that people get out of there at five. It just means that the front doors get closed and we try to hurry up and see the rest of the people so we can go home to our families and start dinners. He felt that if the clinic closed at five, I should have been out at five, and he had talked to me about it a few times before. Thank goodness for me he was never on time.

So it was always after 5:30, but this one specific time he happens to get there about 4:45 and is waiting on me for about ten or fifteen minutes too long. He starts honking the car horn and honking more. He starts driving around the parking lot aggressively, to where I eventually asked the doctor, "Please let me go home, because I don't want to get in trouble." And I tell her to please cover for me and let me go home because the father of my children was outside in the parking lot doing donuts and I was afraid he was going to embarrass me and get me fired.

So she quickly rushes me out the door and tells me to go home and handle my business and to try to be professional and never bring that to work. I knew that that's not what you brought to work. I knew it before she told me, but I knew it even more now that he was outside in the parking lot doing donuts and embarrassing the hell out of me. I quickly make it out the door and lock up behind me, and look at him like he's lost his mind. He's looking at me like he's about to hand me a good old-fashioned whooping because I'm taking too long. I get in the car and sit, buckle my seatbelt, and look at him. I'm not sure if I was angry, afraid, or embarrassed. I guess I looked at him with 1,001 emotions. He quickly asked me to get out of the car and go around the front to the driver's side, where he'd rolled the window down and was try-ing to talk to me from the inside of the car and I'm on the outside of the car. He asked me to get down to his so he could tell me something, and when I do he grabs a handful of hair and starts driving off.

I'm thinking he's just playing. I'm thinking, *Okay, he's going to move a couple of feet up and he'll teach me a lesson and then I'll go back to the passenger's seat and it will be over with and I'll go home, lick my wounds, and I'll be embarrassed that it took place at work, and maybe I'll quit tomorrow because I don't want to come back to a place where I'm embarrassed to work because I was embarrassed by this idiot.* I asked him to let me go, and the more I asked him to let me go the more he starts moving the car. I start screaming to let me go, and I probably said one or two bad words to him, which made him go a little faster and a little further. Before I knew it, he's walking me down the street, the main street that is, Nob Hill, with me on the outside of the car, him on the inside of the car, him holding on to nothing but my hair, and me holding on to nothing but his fist. He's dragging me across the street, reminding me that he's boss and I'm not. He's letting me have a career because he's choosing to let me have a career, but I don't get to dictate to him how he treats me.

By then my shoes are completely scuffed and I'm pleading with him to pull over and let me in the car. We make it almost to Tacos El Rey, which is about a block past Nob Hill, and he pulls over. As soon as he lets go of my hair I start running towards my aunt's house, who lives on Pacific, which is kind of far from there. I don't know why I thought I could make it to my aunt's house. I start running, and the more I run the more he follows me. He rolls his car up on the curb and tells me to get in, and eventually I get in and we drive home. He's got a handful of hair, and I'm just sitting there subdued by him taking me by the hair all the way home. When we get home, he asks me to get out of the car because he's going to talk to me inside the house. I don't want to get out of the car, because I know what's going to take place as soon as I get inside the house.

My son wasn't around. He hadn't even picked up my son from daycare. So I felt like my son and daughter were not going to have to be victims to what was about to take place. I got home and he gave me my belting like I deserved it, and we went back and grabbed our kids, pretended like nothing had happened.

I was so embarrassed to go back to work to the Farmers Clinic. I called in and said I didn't feel well, and then eventually quit in the next few days. I couldn't face Ester. I just couldn't face her. I couldn't tell her that I was too weak to fight back, and I couldn't tell her that he was stronger than I was and no matter what I did I was never going to be as strong as he was.

I decided to apply for another job, which was nice. I went to go work for the State of Washington, and I made really good money working for the Department of Disabilities, working with children that were mentally disabled. Working there taught me a lot, but what it taught me most was great endurance. These children were sick, but I don't think they knew they were sick. Maybe some of them did know, but they didn't acknowledge their disability. They just woke up happy, went to sleep happy, and I guess it taught me that it was all right to be happy even if you were in a crazy situation or if you were in a situation that was outside of your control.

So by now I've worked for the school district, for the Farmers Clinic, and for the State of Washington. The more I work at the State of Washington, the better friends I meet, the better money I start making, and the more independent I start feeling, but I still don't know how to drive yet. So I had to depend on him to take me to and from work. He was just my taxi, and he was my childcare provider whenever he felt like it, because if he was hung over he wouldn't take care of the kids. I'd come home after working eight or sixteen hours to no food, wet diapers, broken things, child spanked, child crying, and just the mess. The more I dealt with this, and the more I dealt with his drinking and doing drugs, the more I picked up on I could do this on my own. I just had to drop the dead weight, which was him.

I worked harder and harder, went back to school, went back to Yakima Valley Community College, went to Central, and finished up some classes that I needed to finish in order for me to continue working in the field that I was headed, which was the Department of Disabilities, or at least that's what I thought at the time. Worked there for a few years and loved it, but then I had an opportunity to go work for Allstate and I took it. Before I went to go work for Allstate, I had made up my mind to completely leave the person that I was with, and I was committed to being successful, and I was committed to making it on my own. I was so committed that I knew that my life depended on me, because he wasn't going to let me go that easy, which meant that I had to fight tooth and nail to get away from him, which meant I had to be prepared for any consequence that came from the act of leaving him.

CHAPTER SEVEN

So here we are with two children. I'm working for the state. We eventually decide to buy a trailer out in Moxie and buy land. So we buy this trailer in Moxie, moved to Moxie, and are doing pretty well financially. At this stage we have all brand new furniture, a nice new home that we just purchased, and a new car. Things seemed to be going right.

He had been sober for probably a couple of years, but when he fell off the wagon he fell hard. Not only did he go back to doing drugs, but he went to doing heavy drugs to breaking and entering people's homes. He was breaking and entering with his cousin, who was a heroin junkie, to breaking and entering into our own home and making it look like somebody else had broken into our own home. The reason he made it look like somebody had broken into our own home was because he sold every last bit of our electronics to the coke dealer in the alley. I wouldn't know that was the guy that broke into our own house, because he made it look like a burglary, and he made it look like it happened at night while we were sleeping. I woke up to make his lunch and as I looked for the microwave I noticed that the microwave numbers were gone. I turned on the light to notice the microwave was missing. When I notice the microwave was missing, I look around to see what else is missing.

I quickly run to the living room and notice that our living room window was completely open, our stereo equipment was gone, our speakers were gone, and the TV was gone. Pretty much every electronic we ever owned was gone from our new house. I call the police and make a police report. They come and take a police report and leave.

Six months later when I'm throwing out my trash, a neighbor that lived out in the alley waved me towards him, and as I came towards him I asked what he wanted, and he hands me a couple hundred dollars. I asked him what it was for, and he says, "Well, your husband came about six months ago and sold me all his electronics, but I was short a couple hundred dollars and he's not come down here since. He waved me down the other day and told me he needed his money. So here's his two hundred dollars I owe him, and tell him I said thank you."

I couldn't believe what I was hearing. What I was hearing was that the father of my children, on top of doing B&Es on other houses with his cousin, did a B&E at his own house just so he could sell his own electronics so he wouldn't have to face me to tell me that he was such a junkie that he sold our electronics to the coke guy down the street. I think he was a coke guy. I don't know what he sold. I'm assuming it was more than coke, because I'm not sure that coke heads sell all their electronics. I know from talking to him in the later years that he was an ice head. So somehow or another he cooked the coke to make it into ice or a rock or something, and then smoked the rock. I don't know because I don't use drugs. I've never purchased coke. I've never seen or purchased rock. I've never been around rock. I guess I was around it when he was next to me. I just didn't know I was.

I bumped into him doing oddball stuff in the bathroom a couple of times. One time I caught him with what I think looked like a lid or a beer lid, a metal lid with some liquid cooking. I'd seen movies, and I thought maybe he was shooting up heroin. When I confronted him about it, he said that it was none of my business, that's not what I thought I saw, and he hit me for asking him what he was doing. I think he was doing drugs. I don't know. I don't care, but I think he was shooting himself up with drugs. Then when the neighbor had told me that he had sold our electronics to him, it just confirmed what I already knew. He was a junkie selling the stuff that I was buying with my hard-earned money. I decided that wasn't going to work for me anymore.

I confronted him, didn't give him the two hundred dollars, but I confronted him and told him what the neighbor had told me, and he said the neighbor was a "f***ing liar" and he was making that up about him, and that he was going to call immigration on him because he knew he was a Oaxacan, and Oaxacans needed to be deported back to Mexico. So he was going to call immigration on this Oaxacan guy. I don't know if he did or didn't. I never saw the neighbor again. I didn't get involved in that. I quickly realized I had to get away from this person who was a junkie. Now it made sense that on certain occasions he took me to his friend's house and made me sit out in the car for two or three hours while he was inside the house doing drugs. I had no choice but to wait for him in the car. If I would have left, I would be in trouble. So I had no choice but to sit and wait on him.

He and his brother hung out a lot, did a lot of drugs together. I was the victim of having to be sitting around waiting for him for three or four days at his brother's house. His brother's wife would be ready to get rid of me after the first or second day, because along with not bringing diapers, we never carried milk. I never planned to stay two or days at somebody's house as a guest because the father of my children left me there and decided to take off drinking for three days someplace else. That was my torture for years and years of being with him, to where I knew I wasn't going to do this anymore. I knew I had to better myself, better my education. I knew I had to make more money. I knew I had to get out from underneath him.

I devised a plan with my comadre Dawn, and I told her that I wanted to eventually leave. By then I had my comadre Dawn and my comadre Neti, which was the neighbor from Fourth Street, who were my close confidants and neighbors. Between both of them, I was able to get a plan together. One helped me with talking to me about what was right and what was wrong, and my other comadre was Mexican who was also undergoing some degree of abuse. Her husband was not abusive like mine was, but he was a macho man that treated her like property, not near as bad as I was being treated. He was able to see what was being done to me, but he was probably not able to see what he was doing himself. He and his wife were willing to help me on more than one occasion.

There was one time when I was stranded in Texas. I didn't just get stranded in Texas. He and I went to Texas with his family, and during an argument, because of something illegal he had done and I didn't want to be a part of it, he went and stranded me out in the desert in Texas and told me, "If I come back and you're here, I'm going to kill you. If I come back and you're not here, I'm still going to kill you."

Once he left me there, I hitched a ride. I called my *compadres* and told them my circumstances. I told them I was stranded in Texas with no money and my children, and they quickly wired me money. His brother came to Texas, picked me and my children up, and brought me back to the state of Washington. They went as far as to rent me a place to live.

Now I have my own place to live, so they were able to help me back to my house. I got back home and continued devising my plan to leave this idiot. He makes it home probably a week or two weeks after I do, and is very apologetic for what he did, and very apologetic for stranding me and the children with no money out in the middle of nowhere in Texas. I, however, had not forgiven him, but knew that I couldn't challenge him, knew I couldn't fight him off me, and knew I had nobody to run to to fend him off me. I had no choice but to let him come back home and stay a bit longer until I could figure out my game plan.

He's pretty much drinking and doing drugs pretty much every weekend, and I'm focusing on work and putting my money away. My *compadre* Don comes and invites us to a function they're having at Amway; it's an Amway convention, motivational and spiritual speaking, all things related to motivational speaking. She convinces us to go with them, which we did. This couple, whose last name was Duncan, were mega-millionaires, and were telling everybody how great Amway was and how great Amway would be for them, and how good Amway was going to be for their pocketbook. This guy was re-inspired to possibly stop drinking and doing drugs so he would get into Amway and make it big, as far as he was concerned. He didn't take into account that in order for you to be successful in Amway you have to be continuously accountable and manage your time properly, which means talk to everybody about Amway and Amway products. Sleep, eat, and drink and be Amway. He thought he could be a drunk and druggie that could clean up and go to an Amway function whenever he wanted to.

This was one function that I really wanted to go to that he didn't make it home on time for because he had been out with his brother drinking and carrying on. He comes home and finds me in a bad mood because I really wanted to this function/convention. In our arguing, he decides to start hitting me because I'm becoming too modern, too about money. I'm becoming a dreamer of sorts, a day-dreamer. He says sometimes daydreamers need to be knocked to their senses. So it was up to him to knock some sense back into me.

In the process of him hitting me, I'm not sure what took place, but I just checked out. I didn't care that he was spitting on me. Looking back, he spit on me for quite a while. When he was done spitting on me, he decides to urinate on me, because he's going to show me how much he owns me, and if I pull away, he'll pull back.

If I yank away, he would become like a rose bush, according to him, or a jagged fence, thorned fence, that would pull me back. He thought I was pulling away and was probably meeting some successful person at this Amway function that I wanted to run off with into the sunset. So he was going to see to it that I not have Amway dreams.

By the time he started urinating on me, I had already pretty much checked out. I was someplace in my happy world, disassociating myself from that situation, that moment. Somewhere in him peeing and spitting on me, he finally gets tired of it and walks towards the kitchen, takes a knife, pins me to the floor, and starts shaving on me because he thinks that I'm some guy with a beard.

As he starts shaving on me, he scared me to the point that I finally just broke down and cried and begged him to let me go. "Please let me go wash up. Let me go to the bathroom and take a shower or at least clean up my face." I had saliva running down my forehead into my eyes, and it was stinging and going up my nostrils.

He finally gives up and allows me to go to the bathroom, lock myself in there, and take a shower and get cleaned up, crying the whole time. Somewhere in my crying, I just decided to go into the medicine cabinet and take a couple of aspirin to alleviate a headache that I had. I woke up in the hospital twenty-four hours later having my stomach pumped. The doctors told me I had overdosed on aspirin. I guess I didn't take two aspirin, I took the entire container. So they had a social worker talk to me at St. Elizabeth Hospital.

At the time I'm maybe seventeen or eighteen. The social worker asks me why did I want to kill myself. I was so ashamed to tell the social worker that the reason I wanted to kill myself was that I felt that was the only way out of my situation, and that when somebody urinated and spit in my face that completely broke me to the point where I no longer wanted to live. He had accomplished what nobody else in the world had accomplished. He had hurt that inner child, the one person I had protected all along. I gave him permission to hurt that small child in me and make her cry, and she wasn't as tough as the rest of me was, and she caught up with me, and I caught up with myself in the hospital. Waking up in the hospital after trying to commit suicide was not where I wanted to be.

I guess the saddest part is not that I wanted to commit suicide, it's that it released me to the man that pushed me to try to commit suicide, because I had been taught that I was not to tell on the person that was hurting me. I was just to say that I was a coward and don't know why I decided to drink the entire container of aspirin, that I had allowed somebody to finally break me. Allowing him to break me was not going to be the answer. It just became that one reference point in my life where I would never let anyone take me back to again. The shame and guilt that I felt I still feel, because nobody, including my mother, knows about it. My children don't know about it. Nobody knows about it but him and I, because he knew I woke up in the hospital, because he panicked and called 911 after I had consumed the aspirin, blacked out, and foam was coming out of my mouth. Not until then did he realize that I almost killed myself.

The worst part of all of this is waking up to the most horrid headache. I had imagined a tsunami siren or a fire siren, or worse. It felt like I had the siren in my head full throttle. So not only was I left with the shame of not being able to fulfill my own quest to kill myself, but the shame to talk to a social worker about why I tried to kill myself and tell her the truth why. I had to be faced with going back home to the person that pushed me over the edge, only to hear that person laugh at me and tell me I was weak for trying to kill myself. He told me not only was I weak, but I was weak and stupid because I was unsuccessful at doing what I set out to do. So maybe that's when he changed my mind about suicide. I was already unsuccessful at doing it, so I don't need to do it again and not to try to accomplish something that is impossible. So I have stuck to doing things that I can accomplish. I'm glad. I'm glad that he laughed at me.

I forgot to mention, in the midst of all of this, what probably caused me to take the aspirin was that when he went to the kitchen and got the knife and started shaving me, he continued degrading me by cutting all of my hair off with this knife. My hair was past my buttocks, and when I woke up from this frenzy at the hospital my hair was shoulder length, shorter than shoulder length. He had cut it with a knife, and I guess when he was cutting it he had taunted me, and I vaguely remember him laughing. I felt like, as he was laughing close to my face and then far away, I felt like a kid on a carnival ride, a merry-go-round that was going round and round and round where I only saw his face a portion of the time, even though his face was always in front of me. I was able to zap in and out to his face and see that frothy mouth and know that the frothy mouth meant he hated me or something about me. He wanted to break something in me, or hurt me. For a fragment of a second I gave him permission, and for a fragment of a second he was able to accomplish me trying to take my own life.

I quickly learned from that experience, and learned that it was just an act of desperation. I believe in God, and God did not allow me to compromise my soul, did not allow me to compromise myself. Maybe when I was knocked out, maybe God himself was able to tell me that there was light at the end of the tunnel. This was going to get better, and that I had the strength in me to beat that coward. I couldn't beat him physically, but I could beat him emotionally, because I felt that if he had no restraint in the things that he did to me, he had no restraint at all. I, however, had restraint, and I was able to turn him off when I didn't want to hear him anymore. I was able to watch his mouth move and not hear a word that came out of it. I outgrew him. I outgrew him real quickly, and I think he knew it. I think he knew it, because he became more hostile and drunk and out of control.

The trailer that we lived in eventually caught on fire, mysteriously caught on fire, and to this day he will never admit to being part of it while in a drunken rage. I got tired of accusing him of it too. I called the fire department, and they weren't able to pinpoint his whereabouts, because according to him and his alibis, he was with them the entire time. I would hate to think that he was willing to set his own house on fire with me and the kids in it, but only he knows that, and he has to live with that, not I. He was so wrapped up in his alcoholism and his drug abuse that I'm sure there's many things he did to me that, even if he tried to apologize, even if he tried to think about things he did to me, there would be so many that he wouldn't know where to start. I would think that he doesn't like to think of himself as the kind of evil person that he was.

When the trailer burnt to the ground, I had no choice but to move into my mom's for a couple of weeks. So he and I moved in to my mother's house for probably less than a month. In the month we were there, my mother had already come to grips with the fact that I was going to be part of his life and he was going to be a part of mine, and even though my mom didn't like the relationship, she didn't want to encourage me to be a single mom with kids.

Her saying was, "It's better to dance with the devil you know than the one you don't." To some degree she was right, because I knew that she couldn't help me out of this situation. She couldn't help herself out of her own situation when she was with Dad, so how was she to counsel me on how to get out of mine? The reason we probably only stayed there for a month was because he can only contain his abuse for about a month, and he was not going to hit me in front of my mother, no matter how much of a coward he was. He couldn't do it. I have a ton of brothers.

They were young and all pre-teens and teens at the time. I'm sure if all of them attacked him at the same time they might be able to take them down. I think it went further than that. I think that no matter how bad he was, he just wasn't that brave or bold to hit me in front of my mom. However, it did not mean that he did not refrain from hitting me at my mom's; he just didn't hit me in front of her, or if he hit me I was not to tell her, because I would get into worse trouble. He was trying to find us someplace else to live, as was I. So within this month, I just decided that enough was enough and I was tired of taking care of him. I wasn't going to live at my mom's and I wasn't going to try to commit suicide, so I needed to figure out how I was going to support myself, when I was going to go, how I was going to do it, and how I wouldn't put myself in a position where I would end up back with him.

I found an apartment on Fortieth Avenue off of Nob Hill, which to me was the good side of town. It was a fresh, new start. So I moved into this apartment, but before I moved into this apartment he and I had a fight at my mother's, where with the strength of having my mom's backing, so to speak, I asked her to tell him to please leave her house because I didn't want to be with him anymore. He had just hit me, and when he had hit me he actually pulled me out of my mom's house in the middle of the night so he could hit me, unbeknownst to my mom, in our car.

So we left our children tucked away in my mom's house. He drug me outside of my mom's front door into his car and waylaid on me in my mom's front yard, and took me into his car and was choking me. What he was famous for was choking me until I couldn't breathe anymore, and release me and blow in my face, slap me around or throw water on me, anything to bring me back to the beating, I guess. Sometimes when he was knocking me unconscious, half the time it felt like God was talking to me and telling me what to do, or telling me, "Don't die, don't die! I'm coming to your aid. Don't die. Wake up!" I always heard "wake up," and when I heard "wake up" I always woke up. I always paid attention to God.

One of the times when he said "wake up" there was—I can't even believe I'm saying this—but there was a police officer tapping the window of the car with the back of his flashlight, and a partner on my side of the car, and me and him in the front seat. He was choking me out, but what the officer paid attention to was probably the fact that he was choking me out. So he came to the car and said, "What are guys doing?" And he told them that we were making out. The officer said, "Why were you squeezing her so hard?"

He said, "No, look, officer, I was holding her like this. I was making out with her. She's the mother of my children, and this is my mother-in-law's house, and we wanted to get intimate outside so we wouldn't be making noise inside my mother-in-law's two-bedroom house."

The officer said, "Sir, this is not the right place to conduct your business. How about you take that back inside the house?" Before the officer could walk away, he turned back and he looked at me, and he said, "Are you crying?"

I wanted to say yes. Then he beamed the light down on the floor and noticed there were some open containers on the floor, and he asked him had he been drinking and driving, and he said, "No, sir. This is my mother-in-law's house. I've been parked here the entire time, and my wife and I were talking about different things."

The keys were not in the ignition. They keys were probably in his pocket, and when he was able to show the officer that he wasn't even driving, that we were just sitting there making out, according to him, the officers walked away, and as soon as they walked away he chuckled and said, "You see? I get to whoop your ass in front of the Yakima police and they don't do anything. This is to teach you a lesson. Look at what they did, nothing but tap on the window and go on their merry way and went right back to having coffee and donuts."

I didn't know what to do with that. I thought, *Wow, if these guys were looking at him choking me, why didn't they take me out of the car and look at my neck and realize that I had choke marks and finger marks probably around my neck?* Not only did I have finger marks, but when I went inside the house, I looked in the mirror and I had blood blisters on my face where he had been choking me out, where he had made vessels break on my face because he was restricting my air. If the cops had really looked at me, they would have seen that he was trying to choke me. Again, they're not mind readers. They had no clue. They were limited to what he and I were saying, and I was not about to point the finger at my abuser when my abuser is standing five feet from me.

So I just accepted that that was one more incident that I couldn't help, one more situation I couldn't get out of. But God was still there, because had they not tapped on the window he might have choked me. He might have accomplished what he thought he wanted. I know he didn't want to kill me. I know he loved me. He always told me he loved me. There were a lot of times he would break down and cry and tell me how much he loved me. When he was in drunken fits, he told me that he loved me more than anybody else in the world. So I felt in his own crazy, distorted way he loved me.

We found a place over on Nob Hill, on the good side of town. I signed the lease for this place on my own, by myself. He was not on it because I felt like, if I had a place with just my name on it, it gave me a leg to stand on if I asked him to leave. I moved to this place without him, and he stayed with a relative at the trailer park. Actually, he went to pick asparagus at Sunnyside, living in the camps while he was picking asparagus, and I told him I didn't want anything to do with him because he was a junkie and drunk and abusive. So he took off and went to pick asparagus, and I went to go get myself a new apartment.

About a month, month and a half, later, he shows up at my front door, telling me he's going to move in, and I'm telling him he's not. I'm telling him this is my own spot. I got it on my own. This is my furniture, this is mine, and he quickly reminded me that it wasn't, that it was ours and I was his property, and he moved himself into the house without my permission.

Even if I asked him to leave he wouldn't. All he would do is make my son cry, because at this stage he's old enough to see that I'm kicking his dad out, and his dad just wants to come home, and his dad is crying and carrying on about how much he loves me and how much he wants to come home and what a changed man he is and how I need to give him another shot for the sake of our children. I tell him that, whether he likes it or not, I'm going to move on without him and I'm going to start dating men. I'm going to find me a future husband, and the only way I can do that is to move on without him, and I'm going to start seeing somebody with or without his permission.

He threatens me and says, "If you see somebody, I'm going to kill you."

I act as if I don't hear him, but I had made up my mind that if I don't move on with my life, I will always have this person coming back to it. At some stage I need some guy to back me up. I need somebody who will defend me against this monster. Eventually I find the guy that I think I want to spite him with, really good looking, sharp dressed, with a really good job.

This guy was newly divorced. It was a business relationship that eventually was going to become more, and I had given up on the father of my children. We were already split up for months, and I had decided that the only way I was going to move out from underneath him was to hurt his feelings by going out with somebody else. If I went out with somebody else, he would be so disgusted with me that he would never come beg me for forgiveness, and never come beg me to take him back, and never want to be back with me. I guess this did work for a while, because he stayed away and bad mouthed me in front of his family and said what a whore I was and how I was doing this and that. I was okay with that, because I wanted him to have a distorted picture of me. I didn't want to be his Picasso anymore. I didn't want to be his work of art. I didn't want to be his property, his belonging. I wanted to be nothing of his, and the only way I could do that is move on with somebody else.

I started seeing another loser just like him and I eventually become pregnant. In my becoming pregnant, he's still coming around and pretending like I'm part of his property. He has forced himself upon me, raped me pretty much, and there's nothing I can do about it because I'm afraid of him. So I tell my new boyfriend about my ex and how he's always threatening me, I can't keep him away, and how I need to move. Can he help me move someplace else, not necessarily with him, but would he help me move away from the father of my children? I didn't know I was pregnant at the time, and neither did he. About four or five months down the road, I go see the doctor because I'm not feeling well, and come to find out I'm pregnant. At this stage, I have to make a decision about how I'm going to face this, because I can just tell him we're pregnant with child number three and move on as if nothing had happened, or I can do what I planned and set out to do, which is let him know I was no longer a part of his life and how this child could be somebody else's child. That would have my image tainted and having him finally reject me forever.

Again, the plan worked for about six months. When I'm about six months pregnant, my mom is pretty upset about the whole pregnancy thing and tells me I need to do what's right, to not have a child with this dumbass, and how I'm going to have a third caesarian, and I don't have anyone to take care of my two existing children. If I died on the surgery table she would never forgive me, and everything I was doing was wrong. I felt lost again, not suicidal, just lost. So I turned to my friends Abel and Nati, who would eventually become my child's godparents. I turned to them for help and they rented me a little place, taught me how to drive, helped me get a car, helped me get a bank account, and eventually moved me out of the apartment that I had just moved into so that he can't find me. They helped me move on with my life. They're limited because they don't have a lot of money, and they don't want to take on way too much responsibility themselves, so I have to learn to carry a bunch on my own, and I do fairly well.

So here I go through my entire pregnancy alone. I have my child, and right before I give birth to my youngest child—probably about seven months pregnant—I'm sitting at home on my rocker, rocking my belly back and forth with my hand over my belly, feeling crappy. Out of the blue, I felt my child caress my arm either with his hand or his foot, but it felt like he stroked my arm with his arm. He made me understand that I was not to be afraid, that God was on my side and that I was doing the right thing for myself, not to consider my son something to be sad about, but to be something I was happy about, because he would give me the strength that I needed to finally walk away from this toxic, poison relationship. When my son placed his sweet little hand on my hand from within my womb, I felt the warmth of an angel, the warmth of God telling me, "Don't be afraid. Don't be afraid to make the right choice, and don't regret the decision to have your son." So I never did. I never looked back, and my child is my best friend, and I'm blessed to have him and he's blessed to have me. It worked out all right, I guess.

By then I'm pretty much off on my own. I meet a young man by the name of Lee, and Lee is so overwhelmed by my child, who is only a few months old at the time, that he asks me to marry him and takes on the responsibility of all three of my children. I didn't agree to marry him, but I agreed to start a relationship with him and get to know him and possibly move in with him and live as a couple before we decide to get married, because I didn't want to fail at marriage. So we lived together for a few years, and everything was wonderful. He was a wonderful guy and loved me to the end of the earth. Maybe that might have been his problem, that he loved me too much, too much to the point where he overwhelmed me and smothered me and choked me and became very possessive over me, very jealous, very insecure. The more insecure he was, the more I was turned off by him, because I was not about to do a second time what I had done the first time, which was live with somebody for ten years in misery.

I made a decision that we part ways, which meant going back to work and getting a career with three children. While I was living with Lee I didn't have to lift a finger. He took care of me financially. He took care of me and my children and treated them like his own. He had a set of twins, Justine and Jennifer, that worked out perfectly in our package, because my kids and his kids got along great. Like I said, we did that for years, and it worked for years, but then when the jealousy factor kicked in, and when the possessiveness and insecurities kicked in, I just could not deal with his emotions alongside mine. So we parted ways as friends. We still left the door open, in the event that I decided to come back into a relationship with him. I eventually closed that door, because I didn't see it fit to hold him in a pause pattern, and it wasn't fair to him, and I wanted him to move on with his life. Eventually he did, and he's happily married now.

I then met another young man that I would date for years. I thought he was my dream come true. I was absolutely in love with him and loved everything about him, loved our relationship, loved his job, loved my life with him. I was willing to spend the rest of my life with him, until he decided to show his colors and turned out to be a chimo, and chimo wasn't going to work for me and wasn't going to work for us. So he went to jail, and I went my separate way and decided that the next person that I lived with I was going to marry. I was not going to live with anybody anymore. I wasn't going to share, and I was not going to share my finances with anybody. So I decided to go about it alone.

CHAPTER EIGHT

I went to work with Allstate, and when I went to work for Allstate I would have to say that was the best work experience. My boss, Dewayne Groth, was one of the best people I've ever met. He's an Honest Eddy, a hardcore Republican who tried hard not to push political agendas onto me, but I believed the more we worked beside one another, the more we realized that we saw eye to eye on a lot of things; our view on religion, police and their job, taxes, on children and upbringing, and marriage and the constitution of marriage. The more he and I talked, the more he made me realize that I would someday be married to a man that I would look up to as my husband, and he would be the leader of the house. He would be the head of the household and not me. I could be his passenger, and I do well in the passenger's seat. I was tired of being in the driver's seat. I was tired of being the navigator, when I had no clue of where in the hell I was navigating to.

After working at Allstate for a few years, learning everything I needed to about auto insurance and life insurance, and becoming very good at it, State Farm comes along and offers me a great job—not just a good job, a great job. So I take this job with State Farm, hesitantly of course. I didn't take the job until I talked to my boss, Duane, whom I felt deserved a fair exit. I felt that he had been the kind of guy that was honest, good, kind, paid me well, taught me a lot, talked to me like a friend and not just an employee. He taught me a lot that I would need in the future and I needed at the time. He and I became great friends and still are, but then I met my next boss at State Farm, who was ironically my drill team teacher when I was in middle school.

So my middle school teacher became my boss in my adult years. He was a good friend. We had a good working relationship, but I outgrew the Yakima office quickly and was offered a job in Seattle. Once I saw my opportunity to leave Yakima and move to Seattle, I took it and ran, moved to Federal Way, Washington, and met my new boss, Rick, whom I had a great working relationship and great friendship with and still do.

My years at State Farm were great. They were great producers of money, great producers of life policies and relationships, some of which are still my friends to this day, some of which who have become greater friends. I enjoyed my life as an insurance agent, and thankfully so, because I was able to sell myself and my family life insurance that I would eventually need in the future.

In 2008, I woke up on the floor of my office, wondering what had happened. I guess I had a seizure that landed me in the hospital, that wrecked my opportunity for continuing my employment because the seizure was the first step to many chronic illnesses to come. This seizure was just the indicator that something wasn't right with me.

And who would have thought that something as minor as a seizure would change the course of the rest of my life. It didn't indicate that it was the beginning of the end. It just shifted my energy in a different direction. It shifted my focus. It made me recalculate everything that I'd done, and how hard I fought to go to school, and how hard it was for me to pass my insurance license, especially my life. Life was difficult to pass. My securities were difficult to pass. I'm faced with the fact that no matter how hard I worked, no matter how hard I studied, no matter how hard I tried to get out from underneath my circumstance, that something else got in the way, or something else interrupted my passage or my journey or what I felt was my destiny to do or accomplish.

So here I am with a big mortgage and three children that are adolescent and pre-adolescent, and I had to figure out how I was going to take care of my family now that I could no longer bring home the bacon, now that I could no longer make the big bucks. So my journey in the disability world was difficult. Navigating through Medicare, going from health insurance that I had paid for to applying for Medicare, applying for benefits that I thought were only available to people sixty-five and older, benefits that I never thought I would need myself because I wasn't sixty-five and over. And even though I was fluent in the insurance business, the health insurance industry and the auto insurance industry are two different industries, and the coverages are completely different.

So just navigating through the first part of my medical expenses was quite difficult. But I think what was even more difficult was sitting at home wondering what I was going to do with the rest of my life, sitting at home and having to think of my life as being shortened in some way, shape or form. I knew that my life had changed when they said I had autoimmune disorder. I wasn't sure what autoimmune disorder meant, but I knew that it just meant that things were going to be different, that my earning potential was over, and that I was going to go back to square one and figure out how to make miracles, how to stretch a budget, how to make money work. Thank God that when this took place my two older children were already off on their own with their own families. My son and daughter had already started their life. So what I had left at home was my youngest child, who is doing fantastic academically and doing fantastic in sports and is in an accelerated program at school. He is part of a very elite group of children that are doing well academically.

He was showing me that all of my investment, all that had been done was starting to reveal itself with my children. My children weren't perfect in any way, shape, or form, and aren't. I don't expect them to be. I expect them to make mistakes just like I made, but I expect them to learn from them, and I expect them to be responsible for themselves and be responsible for their actions. Even if they mess up, they need to be accountable for their doings or wrongdoings or good doings. I want them to flourish academically, economically. I want them to flourish in their community. I want them to be as big and as smart as they possibly can.

So back to navigating through illness and disease: You have to face the biggest threat out there, which is depression and not becoming depressed, not let your old ghosts, all your fears, all your inequities, come knocking at your door at the same time. Being home during the work week didn't feel right. It felt as if it shouldn't be, and I wasn't sure how to wear these new set of shoes. They didn't fit right. I was brought up to work. I was brought up to pay my bills on my own. I was brought up on a non-welfare mentality. I was brought up on my poor mother stretching her apple-picking budget to feed us. I learned quickly through her that you only had minimal and what you needed and no more than. So I'm having to make a decision about this beautiful home that I've worked so hard to purchase, and not only purchase but take two years of my life remodeling, painting, replanting trees, making sure that the outside of my home represented who I was inside, and that was that I was a hardworking person that loved having pretty things.

I was that neighbor that took care of her house, kept the paint pristine, keep the yard pristine, so much so that I would take care of my neighbor's house, my neighbor's yard, so that his yard wouldn't be a reflection on my yard. I've always had really good neighbors. I've been blessed with great neighbors, and every single one of my neighbors, every single one, to this day has become a great influence on my life and is still a friend. I've remained friends with every single one of my neighbors, and every single one of my neighbors saw something in me that they hadn't seen in a neighbor before, and that was that I minded my own business, kept to myself, kept a pretty home inside and out, but also was willing to help my neighbor keep their yard if they were not able to.

One of my neighbors, Sheila, and I always laughed together, because Sheila was the absolute opposite of me. Where I kept my yard pristine, Sheila really didn't care what her front yard looked like, or she was busy working and trying to take care of her family to where she had no energy to focus on her home. So I convinced her to allow me to remodel her kitchen and kind of straighten it up for her, straighten up her house. Then I talked to her about getting her roof done, getting her back deck done, because I told her that her home was her greatest investment and her greatest asset. If she ever needed money in a hurry, she could always use her home as a bank account. We became great friends.

I eventually moved from that house and moved into my next great construction project, creation, remodel, rehab. I would then meet my new neighbor, Linda, who also wasn't about really taking care of her yard, but was a very good sport about letting me manhandle my yard and her yard at the same time so that her house and my house would be the nice houses on the block. The way I figured, I wanted to keep every last bit of my money in equity in my home. I always felt that my home was my pride of ownership, that not everybody was meant to be a homeowner, and I still don't think that everybody is meant to be a homeowner. There are people that were just okay with being renters, or okay living in a townhome or a condo, where they're not worried about their yard or their roofs too much.

Then there are people that are your homeowner's that take care of their yards every weekend. That take care of their roofs and prepare the roofs for the winter, and clean their yards in the spring, and are happy to be homeowners, or happy to wave at their neighbors and be a friendly neighbor, look out for their neighborhood, be part of a neighborhood watch, or at least be part of knowing what's going on with your neighbors, and if they needed a glass of water you're able to provide it. Why not? If they're short milk and you're able to hand them some milk and reciprocate in the future. Why not? Every neighbor I've had, every neighbor I've had, has been my friend.

When we lived in the trailer that eventually burned, there was a young neighbor by the name of Jamie who was a young disabled boy that loved target practice and had this deer in the back of his yard that he would bow hunt with, or aim with his bow and just be out there entertained with his bow and arrow, and entertained with his deer, and entertained with being happy about existing. The child became my friend for a few years. We eventually moved out of there, so I lost contact. We weren't able to keep up with one another, but like I said, almost every single one of my neighbors has remained my friend; my ex-policyholders remained friends.

I've met a great couple in the King County area that would eventually be an intricate part of my life and my success and where I'm at now. The young man and his wife owned a dealership in Burian. They owned a Ford store. When I became ill and wasn't able to keep up with my co-pays because what I'm receiving monthly for disability and what I'm paying out in co-pays are not matching up— my co-pays are greater than my monthly income—out of compassion and friendship, my friend Frank asked me to just come and help him out. He said, "Come help me out when you feel up to it. Do what you can."

He knew I was a great salesperson, so the way he figured is just having me around every now and then was helping me help myself by helping me sell a car here and there, and being able to at least help me pay my medical bills. And what he did is that he never paid me in paychecks, but would take care of my light bill, or would take care of buying me groceries, or take care of paying off medical bills, or help me renew my auto insurance policy.

His wife Nancy was equally nice, and she was just as generous. So much so that my last child, my third child, my youngest child, I was able to make up my will and they accepted the responsibility of taking my child in the event of my premature death. They would take in my son so that my son would continue growing up with their two boys. Who really does that for somebody? Not too many people; not too many people say, "Not only are we going to open up our door to you, but we're going to help you make it through this journey that you're going through, help you navigate through some of the finances. And if you die, if you die prematurely, we will open up our door to your son who's not even a family member." But them even opening up the idea of me not being worried about where my son would end up if I was gone was wonderful.

Not only was I able to leave my son with them, but my sister Virginia was a very intricate part of my life. She was fundamental to my success. She was my nanny for many years. She was the gal that lived with me, took care of my children, was my wife, because I became the head of the household. I became the dad; she became the mom, and my children love her not only as an aunt but love her as an adult parental figure. And knowing that my sister would take on the responsibility of my young child, and my friends also saying they would take on my young child, and his godparents always told me that if something happened to me that they would be happy to take my son and raise him as their own and give him a proper education and proper upbringing and religious background, which was important to me.

It was important to me that whoever I left my child, or my children, to would talk to them about me, and talk to them about God, and talk to them about my mission statement, why I believed the things I believed. The people that were very close to me knew that I believed in hard work, dedication, perseverance, and just more hard work and the ability to fail. The ability to fall flat on your face and shake it off, and get up and move forward and understand that it was just the trial and a tribulation and a stepping stone to where you need to get, to where you need to be, and all it was was motivation along the way, and sometimes it was checking myself. Some things have happened in my past that shaped my future. Had it not happened I wouldn't be able to be the person that I am now. I wouldn't be able to be the nana that talks to her nine-year-old granddaughter about the curse, the big step into being a young lady, without having to disclose some of my own personal mishaps with the curse, the big old period, and how my mother was programmed by her mother not to talk to me about what it would be like to have a period.

My mother just decided that, I guess, I would know about it when it happened and I would know how to take care of myself. But what's even crazier, she always talked to me about my period as if it was some great big curse, as if it was awful. Actually, what she did was she always told me that, because I was a tomboy, and because I was always out and about with my brother, chasing after him, climbing trees and riding bikes and fighting them, one day the curse was going to catch up with me. And pretty much what she told me was that one day, if I continued being a tomboy, that my crotch was going to break so my vajayjay, my personal part, would break and it was going to bleed and it was not going to stop bleeding. I was just going to bleed to death, because that was God's way of punishing us for being adults and because now we are aware of sin. So she told me once you start bleeding it's because you are aware of sin and you have made a conscious choice to know the right from wrong.

So, as luck would have it, I'm riding around on my bike after running around with my brothers and playing marbles with them, and shooting my slingshot, and fighting my brother Salvador earlier about how tough I was and how I could take him down and challenge him. Funny story: this probably was the last time I challenged my younger brother, because I realized he had finally gotten to where he was tough enough to challenge me back, and the fact that I started the curse didn't help the situation any. So I guess I figured out that I could no longer be a tomboy, that I was not a woman, and that because I was not a woman I had to act like one, but of course that also meant I had to challenge my brother for the last time. We had gotten into an altercation earlier that day, and I was just not in a good mood about what had taken place, and I was not in a good mood about having the curse, and I was not in a good mood about the embarrassment that I'd had earlier with the curse.

Because, again, my mother had said that one day my crotch was going to break and bleed to death and it was going to be the last day of my life, when I started my period on my bike, I looked down and am bloody, and I'm on my bike and I had just finished fighting with my brother, so I just felt like okay, well, this was full circle. The curse was coming back to get me and we had company. When I decided to crawl into the house, not walk into the house, I jump off my bike and looked down and noticed that I'm bleeding. So I threw my bike on the cement, crawled my way into the house, cried bloody murder, and made a mockery of myself, because my family was there, and I insisted that my crotch was broken and I was bleeding to death and that my mom needed to take me to the hospital because my crotch was broken and I was bleeding to death. Instead of setting me aside and telling me what really had taken place, they just decided to laugh at me, and my aunt reminded me that that's the reason why I needed to just stick to my mop and broom and SOS and cleaning supplies, because I was no longer a little girl and I was supposed to assume the role of a woman.

Chapter Nine

So here I am at home with one child to take care of, with my entire life happening with a couple of grandkids, and I'm faced with life. I'm faced with what do I do? Is this the end of my life? Do I start living? Do I start dying? Do I become a sick person? Do I fight it? Do I fight it head on? Do I figure out what autoimmune disorder is, what Rheumatoid arthritis is, what disconnective tissue is, and what all the big-ticket items that were coming my direction quickly meant? I only have my teenage son to counsel with at this time, and I feel like I'm burdening him with my emotions, and I feel like I'm looking forward to him coming home from school so that he and I can hang out, so that he can help me navigate through disease, because he's smarter than I am at this point. He's computer savvy and he's Internet savvy, and he's able to kind of help me with what's going to take place, but again he's just a child. He's a teenager. He has no clue about disease. All he knows is that his mom is sick and that he's faced with the possibility of losing me.

So he's accelerating academically. He's beaten all odds and he's in the Cambridge Program at Federal Way High School. He is a varsity wrestler and is showing me that maybe I need to be a little more like him. Maybe I hadn't done too bad. Maybe I was able to talk to my granddaughter and my other grandchildren in a way that I had never been talked to myself.

My granddaughter at this stage is my best friend. Not only is she my granddaughter, she's my little BFF, my little sidekick. We spent the first few years of her life together pretty much all day everyday as my daughter is going to school. And plus, the more my daughter is going to school, the more I figure out just how much I enjoy being a nana, and how much joy this beautiful Lexie Bear was bringing me, and how she was keeping me from being focused on being sick.

All I cared about was hanging out with this young lady and enjoying every bit of her, enjoying every bit of my last child and how easy he was to raise. How, wow, wow, my kid brought me no dramas. My kid was a good person; my kid had been brought up well. My two other kids were doing well on their own and were making me proud. They were lifting the load. My children were reminding me that it was all right for them to not be perfect. It was all right for them to screw up. It was all right for them to make mistakes because, guess what? I had made my own set of mistakes.

So again here I am with this grandchild that is influencing me to move forward. So my granddaughter and I are watching a cartoon one day. We decided to spend a lot of time together and spend it watching a lot of cartoons like *Ice Age*, *Toy Story*, and *Ants*, and *Jungle Book*, and all the Frog tales and Cinderella tales we can watch.

But this one day we're watching *Ratatouille*, and she just looks over at me and she goes, "Nana, that's what you are; you're like that. You're a chef."

I looked at her and I said, "You know what? You're right," and I picked up the phone and called the Cordon Bleu, and didn't just get information about the Cordon Bleu, but I made a decision to go join the Cordon Bleu and graduate from the Cordon Bleu, and not only graduate from the Cordon Bleu, but graduate first in my class, graduate competing, graduate trying to create new dishes.

I had never ever even so much as flipped a burger at McDonald's.

I had not worked in any restaurant at all. All I knew was that I knew how to cook, because I'd been cooking for my brothers since I was ten. Then I went to cooking for my in-laws and, believe it or not, some of the dishes that I made for them that I got in trouble for making then are gourmet dishes now, and they've acknowledged that they weren't prepared to eat food that was more complicated and they didn't know any better. I got in trouble for wasting food, according to them, way back when, and now in my chef years they've all turned back and told me that they knew beyond a shadow of a doubt that I was a great cook.

I have this one story that, I guess … I have a few, but this one particular one when I was only thirteen years old. A couple weeks after I was taken I noticed that one of my sister-in-laws was a fantastic cook; not a good cook, not a great cook, a fantastic cook. She could rock two stones together and call it a soup, and it was the best soup ever. She fed these guys. She lived with this guy from Mexico first of all, and she had two children from two other guys from Mexico, and she was kind of like a stay-home mom. She never worked. She found these guys that would take care of her and take care of her kids. So what she ended up doing was she lived with this guy named Manuel for years and years, and would cook for not only him but his brothers and his friends from Mexico, from his hometown in Mexico. They would come do the seasons, so she rented. Not only did she cook for them and charge them a weekly rate for cooking for them, she also charged them for living in her backyard in a shack or a trailer, a contraption that they slapped together and called a room.

So she would rent them rooms per week, and then she would charge them to do their laundry, and then she would charge them to fix them their lunch. But what she taught me was that she was a great entrepreneur, that she didn't have to work. She was diabetic and was losing her eyesight, but her sense of smell and her sense of housekeeping was fantastic. She was clean. She was very, very clean, and she was a great cook. Well, I was eager to learn from her, and she was not too eager to teach me. She was more eager to show me how good she could cook and how nobody could cook like her, but I guess I saw it as a challenge. I saw it as if she can cook that well, I can learn from her.

So I just stood back and paid attention to her. I paid a lot of attention to her. I looked at the way she seasoned food. I looked at the way she tasted food. I later learned, going through chef school, that she double dipped and it was nasty. She took her spoon and tasted from the pan, and then used the same spoon to continue tasting as she went along with the meal. However, I noticed that she was constantly tasting her food. She was constantly modifying the taste, as she was constantly seasoning it, salting it, and adding more and taking away. If it was too salty, she taught me that you take a potato, peel it, split it in half, and throw it in there; it will eat some of the excess salt and then you can go back to repairing the dish. Not throwing it away but repairing it. She taught me how to repair dishes.

Well, back to this one particular story. She was great in making flour tortillas. She made them all the time, and that's how she packed these guys burritos pretty much all the time, tacos and burritos, but they didn't use corn tortillas; they used flour, and making flour tortillas was completely different then making corn. There was no similarity. There is no similarity between the two. One has hot water, flour, shortening, salt, baking powder, and dough in it, and putting it together and stretching it out with a stick. The other was just plain water, a little flour, and was not any specific temperature. You usually use lukewarm water to make corn tortillas, but everything about them is different. So I paid attention, and I was quickly asked by him to learn how to make tortillas, because that's what I needed to do was make him lunch and make him tortillas.

So I'm thirteen and wet behind the ears. I think I know how to cook, but I don't really know how to cook. I'm just a child. So I asked my mother-in-law and sister-in-law to teach me how to make flour tortillas, and they tell me what ingredients to mix, what ingredients to put together, so I was asked to get a bowl, flour, and add water. Get a pot full of water. Put it on the stove and start it boiling. So I did that. Found the stick to roll out the tortillas with, and found shortening, salt, and baking powder. So I put it all together in the bowl like I saw them do, worked it, kneaded it; kneaded just the flour without the water yet.

So in the process of me kneading this flour, both my hands are in the flour and I'm kneading the salt, shortening, and the baking powder to the flour. And as I'm working this flour mixture, I never paid attention to the fact that my mother-in-law had gone to the stove and took the boiling water from the stove and started pouring it over the flour mixture that I was kneading together, and it took a second. It literally took a second to figure out what was taking place, and then as soon as I kind of caught up with myself, I realized that she was pouring boiling water over this flour mixture, which was becoming very, very, very hot, and very, very sticky, and my sister-in-law starts laughing and tells me start kneading it.

"You need to knead it, because if you don't knead it it's going to burn you," and she was cracking up because she could tell that I was ready to cry or ready to just run out. I was ready to throw the flour in their face, is what I was ready to do, but I couldn't do it because I knew I was going to get hit, and I couldn't do it because I knew it was disrespectful, and I couldn't do it because it was his mom and his sister.

But I felt like doing it, and I pulled my hands out of this boiling, hot contraption and run towards the sink, and start the faucet so I can get some cold water running on my burning skin. They're chuckling about the whole incident, and just then he walks in through the back door and finds them chuckling, and he asked why they're laughing. My sister-in-law tells him that "You took a child that is such a green bird that you should've just went ahead and taken her playpen and her pack of diapers with her, because she can't even make a decent flour mixture to make tortillas."

I'm over the sink running cold water over my hands, crying because I felt like they purposely burnt me. They should have warned me that the water was going to go into the flour. They should've told me they were going to do that, but they didn't. They thought it was funny to just kind of break me in.

I made a decision right then and there that I would learn how to make flour tortillas. When they were not around I was going to boil my own water, get my own contraption going. What I actually learned to do was take a wood spoon when I was pouring the boiling water into the flour, content to take the wood spoon and mix it around quickly, making it stick, becoming cohesive and stick to the spoon, not to my hand. So I would whip the spoon through the boiling contraption fast, aerating the flour, making it so I could stick my hands into the flour when it was still hot but not burning myself; not stick my hands in the dough when it was still super sticky where it would just stick to my skin, but allow the shortening to work with the boiling water, to work with the dough and making it cohesive, making it one, so that when my hands went into it they would still burn, but not burn at boiling temperature, but hot, just tolerable. And I quickly ... oh, I mean I mastered the flour tortilla. I can make a dozen tortillas lickity split.

What I learned was to be efficient. I learned to be fast, and I learned to make them round, and I learned to make them pretty. My first batch of tortillas that I made that were nice and pretty, I knew I had dominated, and I asked him to invite his brother over, because he had an older brother that was good at stringing him along to bad things: to drink, to do drugs, to be abusive. His older brother was very abusive to his wife, who had eight children with him, and he was abusive not only to his wife, but he was also just as abusive to his eight children, and tried to push that upon my babies' dad so that he could be just as abusive to me. He invited him over to show him that he kind of had whooped me into shape to becoming a good wife and a good housekeeper and an excellent cook, and that's, I guess, how I became a chef.

So when I went back to the Cordon Bleu to become a chef, it was probably for my own sanity. It was probably not only because my grandchild had influenced me and motivated me to go back to culinary school, but it was a way to keep my sanity, and it was a way to make sense of how I had adapted to a different food culture when I was with my kids dad's family, but that I'd also re-engineered the way I ate after him, that a lot of the foods that I ate when I was with him I don't touch to this day. I don't like flour tortillas. As a matter of fact, I hate flour tortillas. My last choice of meal would be a flour tortilla, and maybe it's because of the psychological aspect to it. I see flour tortillas as me working in the fields; I see flour tortillas as me being belittled by my in-laws, or my first tortillas being showcased for everybody to laugh about because they were not round. They were *huaraches*, according to them, and they were. They were ugly.

I was a thirteen-year-old kid trying to master the art that women to this day have not mastered. I guess between him and my mother, and my friends Frank and Nancy, who had exposed me to high-end food from Morton's, to the American Grill, to the Ritz Carlton—staying at the Ritz, staying at the best hotels in Vegas—eating at the best restaurants on the Vegas Strip, in Palm Springs, and Cocoa Beach, in all the places that I had the pleasure of visiting, I became a good cook. I was the brokest Mexican, but I also had the pleasure of dining and rubbing elbows with the elite of the elite.

The Ford dealers and all of my friends' friends were influential in helping me continue with my dream of being more than just who I was. If a black man could own a dealership in the King County area—not only one, but two—go from owning one to owning the auction, to owning a second dealership, I knew if a black man could do that, keep his wits about him, be a decent human being, a wonderful husband and father, and a wonderful friend to me and my family, I could go back to culinary school. I could depend on all my friends to make it. I could depend on Chef Mah to not only challenge me, but push me to be a greater chef. Some of the young chefs that I went to school with that were only eighteen or twenty years old did their internships/externships at B-52 in New York had competed in cooking with a friend of mine who runs his own restaurant in Alaska, to competing for Alaskan Airlines meals, to competing for status. I had never cooked professionally.

So I went from never cooking professionally to competing with the best of the best, and learning from the best of the best, and Chef Hess telling me and making that coca face when she says "no fingers-to-face action" or "don't touch your hair." She was our cleaning teacher. She was our professor that taught us about not double dipping, about seasoning properly, about cleaning your area, and all the stuff that I already knew how to do even though I never worked in a restaurant. I was just a clean cook. I was not a chef, and I guess I'm still not a chef. I'm someone who graduated from culinary school and enjoys cooking, enjoys the art of watching people enjoy my food. To this date, I enjoy the art of talking about food, talking about how great being a chef is, how great my second wind is, my second career that I am extremely proud of. I am proud of being a Cordon Bleu graduate, and I am also proud of being an insurance agent financial specialist. I was proud of that. I was proud of someone who worked in the fields and understood.

When I went to culinary school I understood the concept of food, because I picked a lot of the stuff that we talked about. I cooked a lot of the stuff that we talked about. I ate a lot of the stuff we were talking about, because not only did I eat Mexican food again, I was exposed to great restaurants with my friends Frank and Nancy. We ate with NBA players, with CEOs and vice presidents of companies, and like I said, I rubbed elbows with the best of the best. Coincidentally, through Frank and Nancy, I met the man that

I would marry and that would take care of me and challenge me, and that would finally set me at ease. He has taught me that through his own personal experience, through his own personal successes at UPS, through his own forty-year marriage before I came along. He was ready for a challenge. He was ready for a new experience. He was ready for a young wife. He was ready for an eager beaver that was eager to cook, eager to clean. But he was also there for me when I couldn't take care of myself.

He was also there to reassure me, not to make me, but to reassure me that when things got tough and I needed a man by my side that he would be there. He wouldn't just be there financially, but he would be there morally. Along with being there both financially and morally, he is also preoccupied with losing his second wife, and in that pre-occupational state of mind, he sometimes micromanages me or overwhelms me in the sense of overcaring for me, if anything. Maybe I'm not comfortable with somebody taking care of me. I'm not comfortable with completely giving up the reigns, trusting somebody enough to marry them, but this is the only person I've ever married and this is the only person I intend to be married to.

I plan to be successful at being his wife. I plan to be successful at not giving into my disease, not giving into my riddled body, not giving into the Internet. The internet can be great at teaching you about your disease, but the Internet can also be great about over-teaching you about your disease. So I've made a conscious decision, since 2010 till now, not to learn about RA, not to learn about lymphoma, not to learn about COPD, but to learn when people help add to what would be your damaged body. The way I figure it is that my mother added to my immune disorder by being poor, by working in the fields, by not having health insurance, by not applying for medical coupons, because had she applied for assistance we would've had health care, which means I would have gone to the doctor all those years I went to school with a fever.

There were many, many, times I went to school with a fever. I couldn't stay home because I didn't have a babysitter. And because I had to walk my brothers to school, that meant I had to show up to school. The teachers would give me a break. They'd give me slack and let me put my head down on my table when I had a slight fever, but they couldn't keep me at my table and they'd send me to the nurses office so that I could rest there. They couldn't call my mom; we didn't have a house phone. They couldn't call my mom in the apple fields to tell her that I had a fever, so I pretty much stayed in school until it was time to go home with my siblings, and I went home with a fever.

Eventually the school felt sorry enough for me. The Migrant Council put together some money so that I could have my tonsils removed, because I had gone to school for a few years with a fever, with tonsillitis, and the tonsils made it to where the infection ran up and down my throat. I'm sure that that's probably when my autoimmune disorder started, but it wouldn't be diagnosed for years and years to come, but my tonsils were always swollen. I always had a fever, but because we had no money to go to the doctor, my mother resorted to old-school, old-wives' remedies such as having me cut a tomato into pieces, into circles, and put a circle on each side of my tonsils and wrap it with a handkerchief. She had me do the same with the bottoms of my feet, apply Vicks and then a wedge of alcohol—not alcohol, a wedge of tomato wrapped with a cloth that was drenched in alcohol, and two pairs of socks that would eventually, according to Doña Salud, the lady that had raised us when we were kids, break your tonsils. Or you'd go to someone like Doña Salud who would break them, according to them, by rubbing your inner forearm area till they supposedly broke your tonsils.

So that went on for years and, gross but true story, in the middle of the night when I would go to sleep with these tomato wedges on my neck and my feet, in the middle of the night it was uncomfortable because the tomato wedges would stick to my skin. So I would eventually just pull them out from my neckline and just eat it. I guess it's gross because they'd been sitting on my neck the entire time with Vicks, but I guess I didn't care. I'd just eat it in the middle of the night. I never ate the ones off my feet, thank God, but I ate the ones from my neck, and woke up the next morning still with a fever, but smaller grade, and go to school with a fever.

There was this one teacher, Mr. Martinez, who was the guy that would take us to doctor's appointments. He was tied into the Migrant Council, and his job was to take me from Adam's Elementary School to ear, nose, and throat doctors that would eventually operate on my tonsils, ears, and my eyes, because the infection ran up my sinus canal into my ears. The ENT in Yakima had to go in and clean up years of infection, years of scar tissue. I guess the reason I talk about Mr. Martinez was that I felt scared every time I was in his car, in his presence. I think the reason that I was scared—I don't think he did anything to me, at least I don't think he did—was that I didn't trust him. I don't think I trusted him because his eyes were as blue as sky.

I don't know why I didn't trust him, but something told me not to, or to be afraid of him. But he was my ride to and from my doctor's appointments, so I had no choice but to trust him and know that he wouldn't do anything to me; that the school district wouldn't have hired some guy that could potentially hurt a child, or at least that's the way I saw it. So I would counsel myself not to be afraid of this guy so that I could be in the car with him long enough for him to take me to the doctor's appointment, and he's the guy that actually took me to have my surgery for my tonsils and took me to and from the hospital. Again, this was when I was probably eight years old. Now I am really sick with sinusitis and have had polyps removed from my sinus canals—from the back of my sinus canals—and my forehead and my forefront. Sinusitis has riddled me with headaches, migraines, and the after effects of sinus surgeries and wearing plugs in your nose because your nose is going to bleed till the bitter end.

Chapter Ten

Dealing with as many surgeries as I've dealt with, way over twenty, what I've learned is that I do well under anesthesia, and that when you have surgery it's the most refreshing sleep you have. The reason I probably talk about this is that I suffer from insomnia. As a matter of fact, it's two o'clock in the morning now, and here I am recording my book instead of sleeping. I've gone to sleep therapy and sleep studies, and they've determined I just have insomnia that is tied into my chronic illness, which is tied into my terminal diseases, and I guess they give you sleep aids. I take Ambien to sleep with, or to at least knock me out for a few hours so that I don't have to think about the end of my life, so I don't have to think about how hard I've fought to get here to be done at forty-three.

I'm not done being done. I guess I'm not done being me, and I'm not done fighting. I guess this is why I'm writing my book, because I've had two careers that have been taken from me that I worked so hard to accomplish to lose to a disease. I can't be an insurance agent because I'm too sick to show up to work Monday through Friday and work the long hours and the weekends to take pictures of homes and make sure people don't have dogs on their property that they're not disclosing, and look at more vehicle reports and assess premium properly. Although I believed in the company and the company name, I also thought of the policyholder, and I always thought I don't want to just make money from them for a year or two. I'd like to make these people my everything policyholders.

I want to sell them life. I want to sell them disability. I want to sell them boat insurance. I want to sell them everything. I want them to think of me when they think of insurance. Not because I'm making money off of them, but because I genuinely care about their well-being. I genuinely care about their tickets. I genuinely care if they hit somebody, but I also genuinely care if they have just a little tiny accident that they can handle on their own without us raising their premiums. So I felt like it was my job to educate them, not only about insurance, but about self-discipline and responsibility.

I was famous for having my desk clean. It was like a ritual. I would show up to work every day and not pick up my phone for half an hour because I wasn't ready to deal with people. I wasn't awake enough. So I would go to Albertson's and buy myself a cup of coffee every morning, and Rick knew that I wasn't ready to work until I had a cup of coffee in me. Dewayne knew that I wasn't ready to work until I had a cup of coffee in me, and even Eric knew. Eric was probably, out of my bosses, the one that was a little bit harder to work with, but he was still a decent boss. It was just difficult watching people's premiums go up, so I made it my job to educate them a little bit about their insurance, their insurance premiums, how we worked, how we rated you, and how we ran your motor vehicle report after you hit somebody because it was questionable.

If you're out hitting somebody and it's your fault, are you getting tickets? Have you been lead-footed for a while? State Farm loved it that I was honest to policyholders, but they also loved it that I was a little politically correct, because I was that one person that could call a lead foot a lead foot and make a joke out of it and have him put his shoe on top of my desk and check the shoe for lead. I would remind them that I didn't care how many tickets they got, State Farm did. And State Farm didn't care either, because they took two options: to raise their premium and/or to cancel their policy. I wanted them to continue being my friends. I wanted them to continue being in my office. I wanted them to continue being happy about making their monthly premium, and the only way we could both win was for me to educate them on how not to raise their premium, and for them to be honest with me and tell me if they were getting tickets.

So it was a win-win situation, and I loved being their friend. Like I said, a lot of the relationships I have now are a direct result of State Farm and my long-term relationships I made through there and cheffing—well, I never really cheffed.

I did my internship at a catering company that was all right, but I was a little disappointed that I had learned all these chef and cut techniques to not use them. I guess when I went into the restaurant industry, or into the catering industry, I figured out that everything is prefab, pre counted, premeasured, precut. All you pretty much had to do at this place was make it pretty, plate it pretty, and I felt like a bit of a letdown, because I wanted to work in a place like Morten's Restaurant. I wanted to hear the sizzle of a steak. I wanted the butter-over-the-steak effect, and I wanted the broccoli rabe experience, and I wanted the twice-mashed potatoes, and the hundred-dollar ticket. That's what I wanted to do.

I wanted somebody else to enjoy the experience that I had eating at high-end restaurants, and maybe secretly that's why I became a chef. I wanted to eat well and, if I was to be sick, maybe it was my job to learn how to eat better, how to work with my body, not against it, how to feed it the right quantities of food, prepared properly and made pretty.

Through cooking, believe it or not, I've made great relationships. Not only is my husband happy that I am a chef, but I'm his exclusive chef, and sometimes I feel sort of cheated, I guess, because I feel like I don't get to practice my art. I don't get to really flourish as a chef. I've had a couple opportunities to do some great stuff with my cheffing, like taking care of my own wedding, being a part of it, and having Chef Mah and my other chef colleagues, friends, and team-mates take care of my wedding.

My wedding was fantastic, and I thank everybody that was part of it. I thank all of my friends. I thank my friends Tamika and Philip. I thank my dear, dear, dear close friend Mark, his parents, his daughter, his father, and his mother. They were all intricate parts of my wedding, and they were an intricate part of my Cinderella life. It's funny that I even call it my Cinderella life, because I guess it's what it feels like. I live in this beautiful mansion with my hus-band who has accomplished great things, great success, along with my great success, and how I feel like, although my husband is a lot older than I am, he's still open to learning from little old me, and that I'm still learning from him, and that we're still learning that in love, in marriage, in a relationship, in a commitment, there is no such thing as age. There is no such thing as culture. There is even no such thing as religion, because my daughter and her husband have different views on religion. However, he goes to church with her because he knows that that makes her happy. He knows that that fulfills her and her quest to be a good mother and role model to her children.

My husband is very Catholic. My husband grew up in West Seat-tle and went to Catholic school from beginning to end. He gradu-ated from O'Dea Catholic School in downtown Seattle next to the hospitals that saved my life, next to my favorite hospital, Virginia Mason. I feel as if it's this beautiful, full circle of imperfection blended with perfection. So my circumstances have been imperfect. Everything I've lived has been imperfect—everything—my aunt being mean to my mother and kicking her out into the street, forc-ing my mother to find us a place to live in a few days, forcing my mother to get a job in a few hours, forcing my mother to learn. My mother's sister forced my mother to grow up. My bad situations forced me to grow up, and I'm thankful to each and every single person—even the ones that hurt me—that were a part of my life.

One of the best people I've met in my life passed away in the last year. I'd like to talk about my girlfriend Yolanda, because she was beautiful, energetic, and full of life, vinegar and spirit, all that good stuff. Ironically, she was a Taurus just like I was and, ironically, she had been taken at a young age by a guy with the same name as my guy's name. She was also from Texas, also young, also worked in the fields, also migrated towards Washington through Idaho through the potato-picking experience, and, ironically, she and her brother became very successful dealers. That's how I met her. I worked selling cars briefly while I was going to school as an attempt to make money quickly, because I could sell ice in a blizzard in Alaska. I guess my old saying is that "I could sell ice to an Eskimo in a blizzard and show him that this was the best ice he had ever had. That this ice was not just like any old ice, but this ice came with a nice set of gloves to keep him from freezing his hands, and this ice was cleaner than the next ice and better than the next ice."

So I guess I learned that selling myself was pretty easy, selling my idea was pretty easy, and because I believed in what I did and in myself, I never sold anything I didn't like. I never got involved in Amway. I never got involved with pyramids. Everybody wanted me when all the pyramids and the little scams came into play; everybody wanted me to be a part of them. Everybody wanted me to be a part of Pampered Chef, be a part of Amway, be a part of Kitchen Fair, be a part of this, but I was never interested. I was never interested in that, because I felt that it took too much energy to build a client list, and I wasn't ready to hear a whole bunch of nos. Ironically, when I was an agent with Allstate, my boss Dewayne explained to me that for every hundred nos there is going to be a yes. And don't worry about the nos, because the yes is going to be a firm yes, and it's going to be a good yes, and it's going to be a financially advantageous yes. So he taught me that no didn't mean no, it just meant no right now.

So back to me being an agent with State Farm. I was great at what I did because I never sold anything I didn't believe in. I never talked about anything I didn't believe in. So selling life insurance was easy for me because I had a story, and my story was that my father died, left my mother widowed with seven kids to take care of, and he was nowhere to be found. He was dead. He checked out. He went and got himself killed and left my mother holding the bag, left her holding the entire responsibility, left her to fend for herself, and left her to be belittled, hurt, abandoned, pushed, laughed at, and ridiculed by her family—the people that should have helped her because they were here. They had already caught on the American way. They had already caught on to the language. They had already caught on to education.

My Aunt Teresa was in high school. She graduated from Davis, but my Aunt Teresa, believe it or not, was and is the nicest of my family members. She was neutral. She never got involved in any of the politics, and still doesn't. My Aunt Teresa is a wonderful gal who loves hanging out with me and my children and my grandchildren, and I appreciate her for that. My Aunt Teresa, my mom's sister, has been a great person for my mother to have. She's kind of like the only person in her corner—well, not really, because she's got some uncles. She's got my Uncle Pueblito who was my grandpa's brother, and my Uncle Salvador. She's got a couple uncles on her dad's side, and even some on her mom's side, that love her and always saw her as a victim, a victim of circumstance, a victim of her family.

Like I said, my Aunt Nancy, my uncle's ex-wife, is the gal that brought us back to this country. She took it upon herself to drive to California, pick us up, and drive us home to what would be bittersweet. That would be us coming back home to the people we were supposed to know, but weren't really familiar with, that would eventually show us that we were on our own, that we had nobody in our corner but our mother. So no matter how much my mother hit us, no matter how much she insulted us, and no matter how little she knew about raising seven kids, she did it. She did it on her own with help from nobody. So my mother is my shero. She is the gal that I get to help now, help her navigate through her disability, help her navigate through her riddled body. My mother's arthritic; and she's arthritic because she showed up to work for over forty years. She showed up to her same place of employment for over thirty-three years and she never complained.

My mother was Doña Mari, the lady who gave all the other ladies from work a ride to and from work. Ironically, the lady who did not know how to drive ended up being everybody's taxi and, again, like I said, my mother is my shero. There is no such a thing as a hero—there's sheroes.

She also taught me that there is no such a thing as superheroes—well, she and my brother Sal—because my brother Sal and I were getting into a fight once, and I don't know why, but I asked my brother to wait. I wasn't ready to fight him in my regular girl clothes, so I asked him to wait, and he chuckled—and it was like I don't think he had a clue why I had asked him to wait. I went back to my bedroom and put on a Wonder Woman outfit so I could fight him with my superpowers. When I returned in that outfit, he took one look at me, chuckled, then punched me square in the face. He said, "There is no such thing as superheroes. Go back and put on the right outfit to fight me with."

I went back to my bedroom, put on my Converse, my overalls, my baseball shirt and my baseball cap and came back looking like a tomboy, which was what he was used to seeing during an altercation, and I punched him right in the face. I told him, "There is no such thing as superheroes but there is such thing as Wonder Woman." We both sat there crying and my mother walked in and asked why we were both crying and we didn't reply. We just sat there with each of our eyes swelling and dealing with each others emotions and we were being friendly with each other and comforting each other and not telling my mother that we had just fought.

CHAPTER ELEVEN

We grew up on TV. TV was our biggest, best babysitter. My mom was working in the fields. I was the babysitter, and I knew nothing about babysitting. All I knew was to turn on the TV and that I had to have the house clean when my mom got home, because if not I'd get spanked. So I manipulated my brothers into helping me clean the house, without them really knowing they were helping me clean the house, because my brothers weren't allowed to clean the house. They were boys. I was the girl. It was my job to clean, it was their job to work or clean the yard or help my mom with guy-like chores. So they were adamant not to help me do girl jobs, and my brother Sal was the one that always challenged me, but he was also the one that was my favorite person and still is. He's the one that I got along with best, between my sister Virginia, who was always in my corner, and my brother Salvador, who was a comedian.

The rest of my brothers and I had a very good relationship, and still do, but a little bit different than them two, because them two were the two that I think understood and understand me the best, and them two are the ones that I argued with the most. Virginia, like I said, was not only my sister, but eventually came to live with me because my mother wasn't really good at taking care of her needs and my brothers were bullies to my sister. So I eventually asked my sister to move in with me when she was about thirteen years old, because I was tired of seeing my brothers bully her. Not only did my brothers bully her, but my mother had the great idea to let my sister live at my grandmother's house for a couple of years, and my sister became my cousins' mat of some sorts.

My grandmother had taken in this child that had been given to her by her stepsister, and this child was like the golden child. She could do no wrong. She was perfect and she was beautiful. She was meant to be a supermodel and all these great things because she's beautiful. I can knock on her about a lot of things, but I can't knock on her about her looks. Her looks are above a bunch of folks' looks. She's very pretty, but pretty doesn't make her nice. Pretty has just made her manipulative, and she's manipulated my grandmother and taken advantage of my grandmother's illiteracy and inability to take care of herself and her stature. My grandmother is only about four foot three or four and weighs about a hundred pounds. So my grandmother is not much of a woman and doesn't have much of an education. She worked her entire life in the fields, and she was also a victim of my grandfather. My grandfather was very abusive to her and her young.

We have this repeated history of women being taken as little girls by men who are much older than them who treat them horribly. So my grandmother was an abuse victim from my grandfather who took her as a child. They immigrated to the United States in the early 60s when my mom was only about six years old, and my grandfather dies and leaves my grandmother widowed with four children—and that's not counting the two that had died in Mexico—but he's left her widowed with four, and then my grandmother takes on this other child that, like I said, was given to her.

My grandmother never adopted this child; she just took care of her, and we treated her like she was family, like she was my grandmother's daughter. Eventually she knew she wasn't my grandmother's daughter because people always talked about it secretly. Then, not only did people talk about it secretly, but her father used to come and see her when she was a young child, and they were ashamed of him because he was just this poor Mexican guy that worked in the fields who didn't even own a car, who rode around on a bike in town. So my mom's baby sister never acknowledged him as a father. I guess she kinda sorta does now. She knows that that's her dad.

When she turned fifteen years old her mother tried to come back into the picture and pick up where she had left off. She had forgotten that she had not only abandoned her in my grandmother's house, but she had also given away her siblings, her sisters. This lady had given away all her daughters, but somehow or another kept her sons that she would have in the future. So she had this thing about hating her daughters, and didn't come into my grandmother's daughter's life until she was about fifteen years old. By then it was too late, because my mom's baby sister resented her biological mother, and I don't think had an emotional bond towards her like she did my grandmother. She saw herself as my grandmother's daughter, but that didn't keep her from being abusive to my grandmother, and hasn't kept her from being abusive to my grandmother.

She's just learned from my aunt, my mom's other sister, my Aunt Connie. My Aunt Connie taught her how to be abusive, because my Aunt Connie was abusive to my grandmother throughout her teenage years, and even after her teenage years. When my aunt married her first husband, my grandmother moved in with her and her husband, and worked in the fields and they took her paycheck. So my aunt and uncle cashed my grandmother's paychecks for as long as my grandmother lived with them. As a matter of fact, they bought a house in Mexico with my grandmother's money that would eventually be lost. My aunt eventually got divorced after about twenty-five years of marriage, and the woman that my uncle was cheating with on my aunt was my aunt's best friend, her childhood friend, and they took their property in Mexico. They took my grandmother's property and my aunt's property in Mexico, and my grandmother is eighty-something years old and has nothing to show for her fifty years of work.

She has absolutely nothing to show for all of her effort, because she owns nothing. Even the house that she lives in, which is in her name, she doesn't own, because my mom's baby sister owns it. She's gotten my grandmother to quick claim it to her and give her something showing that she is the legal owner of the house when my grandmother dies. So, ironically, my grandmother has worked her entire life, and what little she's able to attain is not going to go to her biological children. It's going to go to this child that she helped her stepsister raise. But it's none of my business. It's not my stuff. I just feel that my mother got kind of shortchanged, because my mother has been taking care—had, past tense—had been taking care of my grandma through the last eight years.

My mother decided to sell her house, I guess as a psychological thing. I think my mother wanted to mend her relationship with her mother by taking care of her mother in her older years. So my mother sold her house to go move into her mother's house to take care of my grandmother. The funny part was that for the eight years my mother lived at grandmother's house taking care of grandmother, my mom's younger sister was getting paid for it. I don't know how that happens, but it does happen. And then my mom's younger sister decides one day that she's going to kick my mother out of my grandmother's house. So she gets home from work one day, takes my mother's belongings, and throws them outside into the street and tells my mother that she has to move out.

My mother has been living with my grandmother over seven years, going on eight years, and taking care of my grandmother for going on eight years, and her stepsister, or younger sister, I guess decides out of nowhere that she is going to kick my mother out so she can move in with Grandma. It sounds like her now marriage is going to the garbage bin, so she's looking for a place to live, which is at grandmother's house. So first she kicks my mother out of her mother's house, then moves in her daughter into grandmother's house. Her then teenage daughter who's going to school is my grandmother's roommate and is having friends come over, so my eighty-something-year-old grandmother is having to live with a teenager, who's living like a teenager and acting like a teenager, and is forced to bite her tongue and not say anything about her grand-daughter who she loves.

She loves her granddaughter more than she loves anybody else, more than she probably loves any one of us who are her biological grandchildren, because she raised this granddaughter. So my mom's younger sister has moved her child in, and now is going in the process of moving herself into grandmother's house, and out of nowhere she just gets rid of all of my grandmother's belongings, just discards them. Doesn't ask my grandmother can she get rid of them. Doesn't ask her opinion on it, she just discards my grandmother's belongings and brings in new belongings, which my grandmother's responsible for paying half of the stuff, and part of the stuff I think is hers. I don't know and I don't care, because I don't get into my grandmother's business, but I believe that she moved in nice furniture because she couldn't live not only in the bad side of town, but she couldn't stand to live in the bad side of town with ugly belongings. So she cleaned up my grandmother's house and made it pretty, and aesthetically it was pretty, so that Grandmother could see that she had nicer things, or that they could just live more comfortable.

What I realize, looking at my mother's relationship with her mother and how her mother didn't bother to call the police when she was taken at the age of twelve from California, is my mother did exactly the same thing with me. She didn't call the police when I was taken at the age of thirteen, and I think I was damned to have my own daughter probably leave at the age of twelve or thirteen. Thank God she didn't, but she was also a young mother. So it's like having the curse of being Mexican meets the curse of becoming Westernized or Americanized battle one another.

So my daughter went off and had her family young and decided to be a young bride and a young mother like I did, like my mother did, like her mother did, but every generation got older and smarter, so I was able to protect my daughter for a little bit longer—not too much longer, but longer than I had. I would have liked her to get married after her twenties, but she got married young and had her family right out of high school. Like I said, it wasn't the ideal way of doing it, but who was I to tell her not to do what I had done, and what my mom had done, and her mom had done. How do you break a trend that has been going on?

Well, I guess you break it by acknowledging it, and by acknowledging that it wasn't right and it isn't right, and that when my granddaughter is a teenager I've already preprogrammed my nine-year-old granddaughter to know that she's not to get married young. She is to graduate from high school and go to college, and if she wants to date a couple boys from high school through when she decides to get married, it's probably best that she does. It's best that she learns who she doesn't want to marry before she just marries the first knucklehead that comes along who proposes marriage to her. I don't want her to give up her youth. I don't want her to be a young bride. I don't want her to be a young mother. I want her to have the American dream, which is finish high school, be involved in all the high school activities, sports, and go to college. Be involved in all that college has got to offer—maybe not all of it. I don't want her to become promiscuous in college I just want her to experiment with some of the stuff that takes place in college, and I see it because my son is at the University of Washington.

I see what happens to young girls straight out of high school to sorority houses, trying to discover their own bodies and themselves, and with parents aren't there to micromanage them. Mom and Dad aren't there to keep them in check. They can drink and they can go to frat houses and act stupid. With today's You-Tube and Internet mentality, it scares me to think of my grandchild in college in the future, with Lord knows what technology. Will she compromise herself? Will she put herself in a position that she is forced to make the decision because of the way she sees herself, or the way she views her split-second decision to put something on the Internet that she should not have, or whatever source of information is available then?

I'm not going to worry about it now, because she still has nine or ten years before I have to worry about it, and sadly I'm probably not going to be around for that. Sadly, the only thing that my granddaughter will have to hold on to is going to be the sound of my voice in her head telling her that nana loves her and that nana believes that she can be everything that she wants to be—just like she inspired me to become a chef, just like she inspired me through Ratatouille that I could be that chef. I was a chef, and this creature believed in me 110 percent, so I believe in her. Not only her, I believe in all my grandchildren. I believe in my children. I believe my son will graduate from medical school and be a great doctor. I believe that my older son, in spite of his mistakes, will be a great welder, and he's a great husband. He is a great father, and he makes mistakes like the rest of us, but he's learning. Not only is he learning, but his heart is filled with love and compassion, and he is the most loving creature I've had the pleasure of being around. I love being around my children.

I'm forty-three years old, and my twenty-nine-year-old son is my best buddy. He's this big, buff, heavy, needs-to-lose-some-pounds guy, who's this big teddy bear, and although I wish he didn't have a lot of influence from his father, he does. I don't want him to hate his father. I don't want my children to resent their father. I want them to understand that their father was young when he did what he did to me, and their father made me who I am. Their father was very important in the person that I've become. So through his trials and errors, I've become who I am, and ultimately I forgave him, and I guess this is what it all comes down to. This book comes down to me practicing ultimate forgiveness. I have forgiven, and I will continue to forgive everybody who's ever hurt me, everybody who couldn't do anything to save me, everybody who looked the other direction when they should have helped a thirteen-year-old kid.

But I have also forgiven the father of my children, because he is just that the father of my children, and he was a victim of his own circumstance. Like I said early on in this book, the reason that he was the way he was to me was because he was a victim of abuse himself and he didn't know any better. He didn't know to go to a counselor. He didn't know to go to therapy, and he didn't know that it wasn't his fault, and I forgive him. I forgive him for everything he's ever done to me. I forgive him for every time he's ever slapped me, and for every shred of dignity he took from me. I forgive him for making me who I am. Thank you and I forgive you, and I forgive everybody who's ever hurt me or anybody that I love.

I think I'm a difficult person to love; as a matter of fact, I know I am. I know I look at the way my husband looks at me, and I know that he loves me. I know that there's nothing he wouldn't do for me, but I also see that I'm a difficult person to love and that he's conflicted with rationale, with knowing that he loved his first wife for forty years the way he did, and knowing, or I remind him to please not compare me to his first wife or his first relationship, because I'm nothing like that. I'm totally different. She was she and I am me, and I don't expect him to understand what I've been through. I don't expect him to reason with what I've been through, but he is so protective of me, and he is so wanting to fix my past that sometimes he overwhelms me. He overwhelms me because I don't know what to do with all this emotion. I don't know what to do with his sense of urgency to rescue me and protect me from everybody, or shield me from everybody, and I find that the more that he tries to shield me, or the more that he tries to protect me, the further I'd like to push him, because I don't know how to depend on somebody. I've never been taught to depend on anybody.

I've always known to depend on myself. My older son, my Jesse, tells me this, and when he tells me this, and within the last few weeks, I've made a decision to accept my illness, to embrace it, but to also learn about it. Learn how I can stop it. Learn how I can prolong my life. Learn how I can prolong the quality, not quantity, because I know that the quantity part is not going to be there, but make it quality. Make every day when I get up the best day ever, the best day I possibly can. Rheumatoid arthritis and chronic illness makes it to where it's difficult to get up with the right frame of mind, when your body is screeching like a tin can. That's my ongoing joke; that I am headed down the Yellow Brick Road to see the Wizard of Oz, and I'm the Tin Man, and I'm the Scarecrow, and I'm Dorothy, and I am everything about the Wizard of Oz.

I am looking for God and for acceptance, and I'm looking for permission to be sick. I'm looking for permission to vent, permission to be upset about being upset about being cheated, but that doesn't make me a victim. That just makes me somebody who's dying, who's venting about dying.

My son, my Jesse, says to me, "Mother, I wish I could show you, I wish I could tell you, I wish I had the proper words to tell you, just how appreciative I am for everything you've done for me; how appreciative I am for everything that you've taught me; how appreciative I am that, even though you are deathly ill, you keep getting up, and that you keep smiling, and you keep singing, and that you keep challenging me and challenging us to move forward."

The biggest challenge I have with my children is helping them accept my death.

In the last few months, I've had to open up to my family and show them with my medical records just how chronically ill I am. I guess telling my mother that I'm dying is difficult because my grandmother is healthy. Not the healthiest person in the world, but she's an eighty-five-year-old gal that doesn't take medication. So she's healthy as far as I'm concerned. She's healthy for somebody who worked in the fields. She's extremely healthy for somebody who was abused by her husband, and she's even healthier because she's never been independent of her children. My grandmother was a victim of her husband, who controlled her, and then became a victim of her daughter, who will continue to control her, and I don't think my grandmother has ever had a voice. If she has, it's been a voice of discontent and sometimes bad words, which is kind of funny, because I think of my grandmother as dying, and I don't want to see my grandmother dying, cussing, or defending herself, or having to call somebody out of their name out of desperation, sincere fear, or out of frustration.

The frustration that she's eighty-something years old and can't fend for herself I would imagine feels like what a forty-three year old that is dying and can't fend for herself feels like. So I see eye to eye with my grandmother, and I feel compelled to feel compassion for her, and I forgive her for not being there for my mother. I forgive her for not being there for us. She never babysat us. The people that ended up babysitting us as children were strangers. The Avon lady, Josephina, and her husband riddled with Parkinson's. Josephina, although we only lived at her place for a few months, was an abusive old lady, but she was also nice because she opened up her house to us.

So even though she fed us rotten food, even though her husband was a nasty guy with Parkinson's, even though she cut my hair without my mom's permission, and my mom wanted nothing more than to kick her ass for cutting her daughters hair, she was good to us. In Mexican culture, you don't cut your daughter's hair, first of all. Secondly, you're not the babysitter who cuts your daughter's hair. My mom moved out the day the lady cut my hair, and that's when we moved into Doña Salud's, who turned out to be not only a great person, a great babysitter, but she turned out to be the grandma we didn't have. She turned out to be the family member we didn't have, and her husband Don Cheque, was a nasty old perv, but thank God he didn't live with her year round. This guy had a wife in Mexico, and I think he had a wife in California somehow, and Valdo, the kid that this lady was raising, was not even her kid. He was a kid that her husband brought her from Mexico from the wife he left behind in Mexico.

So Doña Salud was this guy's lover and ended up raising one of his children that he had with his official wife in Mexico. It was just a twisted, crazy mess, but this child, Valdo, turned out to be an absolute brat, an overentitled person that would abuse Doña Salud. He would abuse her to the point where he was a gambling addict and, I believe, used drugs and eventually set his house on fire—I think to get insurance money—and put this old lady in a nursing care facility in Wapato, where I was determined to find her, and I did. I found the lady that took care of us with no requirement. We weren't related to her, so it wasn't her job to take care of us, but something she said to me as a child stuck with me, to where I had to find her as an adult and thank her for taking care of us.

Grandma Taylor was also a lady that took care of us. Grandma Taylor took care of us for years. Not only did she take care of us, but she took us to church in her little Pinto wagon. She crammed all of us in the little Pinto wagon, and then her husband James died and she looked to us to comfort her. We were her family. We were there; we went to church with her. We helped her bury him and we comforted her, because she was our grandmother. She was our white grandma who ran a daycare facility and took very good care of us, and Doña Salud was also a lady who had no children, who maybe had adopted us as her family. Between them two ladies, I guess my mom was blessed, because between those two ladies, both of them were instrumental in helping us grow up.

Like I said, Doña Salud told me something that stuck with me forever. When I was a child, maybe about seven or eight years old, we lived with her on Third Street. She'd send the boys off to go play, and her nasty husband was back in California with one of his other wives. She sat me in the kitchen as she made tortillas, and when she was done making the last tortilla, she sits right next to me, turns me over, looks at me, and she says, "Don't be sad when your aunt ..." My mom's sister Connie was notorious for calling my mom a prostitute, a whore, and how she had to sell vajayjay to feed us, and how when my sister and I grew up we were going to be whores just like my mother. She did that throughout my childhood.

She rarely came to our house, but when she did come with Grandma, they would just shrug their nose and tell us how dirty our house was and how poor we were. She was really good about telling my sister and I how someday, if we didn't take care of ourselves, we were going to be whores just like my mom, and the only thing we had to bargain with, the only bargaining chip we had was our kootch, and how are our kootch was going to be the thing that paved the way for us, and how my sister and I were both going to live at home with my mom and have dozens and dozens of children. Ironically, neither my sister and I have ever gone back home with children.

When we had our own children we've been responsible for our kids from that day forward. But I thank my aunt. I thank her because she put that in my head that you could never come home. That I would never give her the pleasure of coming back home so that she could tell my mom you see I told you so. So I made it my job never to come home after I had children, but Doña Salud told me that, in spite of what my aunt said, I could grow up and be a young lady, as long as I respected my body. I think she knew her husband was a chimo. I question whether or not she knew, but she hugged me and she said, "Don't ever let nobody touch you anywhere you don't want them to, and if they do you can come to me and tell me. It's your body. Don't let anybody touch it. Don't let anybody do to you what they're not supposed to." I loved her for that.

I loved her for hugging me, and I found her when she was in a nursing care facility just so I could thank her for being an instrumental part of my life, for taking us in, for talking to me about certain things that nobody else talked to me about; just the same with Grandma Taylor. I found her in the later years of my life, when she was old and ready to die, to thank her for being our adopted grandmother. Even though we didn't have a grandmother growing up, we had enough surrogate grandmothers that it was all right. It was all right to not grow up in that environment that I was so scared of, not to grow up with my aunt insulting my mother. Not only did my aunt insult my mother, but she got my mom's cousins to get in on it, to talk about how if my mother ever wanted a man to be by her side, he had to be man enough to bring a fifty-pound sack of mesa so that we would have enough tortillas to eat, and a fifty pound sack of rice and beans. They weren't providing us with food, so I don't understand how in the hell they were concerned about how we were going to get fed, because none of them so much as bought my mom a gallon of milk.

As a matter of fact, growing up we didn't have milk. We had powdered milk because we couldn't afford real milk. The government was giving out cheese for a while there at the state fair, and I remember my mother not wanting to go get cheese, because she saw that as going on welfare. I persuaded her to go get on the cheese line, because we wanted cheese. We were sick and tired of not having cheese. So my mom stood in one line, and I stood on another line in the cheese line, so I figured I could carry one or two big bars of cheese, and she could carry two. All of a sudden, we had government cheese and could have quesadillas and enchiladas at home, and we could just have cheese and powdered milk, and it felt like we were normal. We had normal food in our house.

Going to Grandma's house was weird, because it always felt like we were walking into a museum that we were not welcome to, that we weren't allowed to touch anything, we weren't allowed to sit anywhere. Not only was my aunt real stringent about that, but her husband was even a worse asshole than she was. My Uncle Daniel would just look at you and look at your hands as if you had something to put in your pockets. They made us feel very uncomfortable, so we rarely went to Grandma's house. My mom's baby sister was a spoiled brat, so she'd invite us over whenever she felt like playing with somebody. As soon as she was ready to be done playing with you, all she had to do was tell you to leave the house, or start crying and pretend like you had hit her so that my grandmother would ask us to leave.

I guess I didn't know that she wasn't really my grandmother's daughter, but I always felt like why does my grandmother kick us out of her house? Why does my aunt kick us out of her house? Why does my uncle look at us like we're there to eat up his house and steal something from them? One thing we had been taught early, early, early, early on in life was that if you stole something my mom was going to kill you with a whooping. Not only was she going to spank you, she was going to really get you. So we knew better than to steal anything. As a matter of fact, I took something from Mervin's because my cousin Fidel was a thief, and we knew he was a thief. Everybody knew he was a thief. Him and his brother Pachito were thieves. So they always talked about them like, "Stay away from. Don't be like so-and-so thief, so-and-so's child who's a thief."

My family was really good about letting you know who was on drugs, who was a thief, who was broken up, and who was promiscuous and who wasn't. The gossip, the whole *chisme* novella growing up is how we grew up, your typical Mexican novella family. I figured, "Hey, if my cousin has new stuff and he doesn't have to buy it, why do I need to run around with patched-up pants?"

So I decided to play the cousin part, and Veronica and I decided to go to Mervin's and go steal something. She and I decided we were going to go to the store and we were going to steal pants, and we were not only going to steal something, but we were going to blame it on my cousin Fidel. So we get home after stealing clothes, and we get on my aunt's roof part of the house. We got to the second part of my aunt's house, went out the window, played on the roof for a while, and decided to come inside and try on our new clothing.

Well, in the process of trying on our new clothes, my aunt notices that we've got a bunch of new clothes we didn't buy and she didn't buy for us. So she quickly snatched us up and put us in the kitchen and asked where we had gotten our clothing from. We had already talked about who we were going to blame it on, which was my cousin Fidel. So both of us blame it on Fidel, and as luck would have it, he never came over because they didn't trust him because he was a thief. He never came over to my aunt's house. He came over that day, and my aunt was trying to talk to him about not influencing us to be like him, not influencing us to steal, and he's looking at her like he doesn't know what the hell she's talking about. He didn't steal the pants—Veronica and I did—and it didn't take very long for my aunt to figure out that he had not stolen the stuff for us, but that we had taken it upon ourselves to steal, and not only steal but blame it on him.

So my aunt was quick to call my mom to come over, because she needs to tell my mother that I'm a thief; not so much that Veronica and I are thieves, but that I am a thief and that I encouraged Veronica to do it. Whereas Veronica encouraged me to do it, and because she could get away with murder, we just did it. We had to take the stuff back, and my mom beat the hell out of me and reminded me and taught me why stealing wasn't what I was going to do. I never did it again, so I guess I'm glad she taught me that stealing was not where it's at.

I can hear my mom in the back of my mind, "Don't take anything that's not yours, and even if you don't know you took it, God knows, the people know, the stores know." All this and all that my mom taught us, I guess. My mom taught us that we needed to have a moral compass, that even though you weren't there to reel yourself in, you should let your moral compass do it for you. Ironically, my husband is the same way.

My husband is a devout Catholic and goes to church every Sunday. I go to church with him as often as I can when I feel well, but there's a lot of times when he goes to church at eight o'clock in the morning, and I just don't feel like getting up at eight o'clock in the morning to go to church. I feel like I haven't sinned at eight o'clock in the morning, and I feel that he's doing it because it makes him feel better. It's just routine, and it isn't so much that he's looking for comfort in Christ, it's that he's so used to doing it from Catholic school that it's just become routine to go to church early in the morning. I don't go to church every Sunday, and I don't go to church early in the morning.

I, however, go to church when I feel like God and I need to talk. I need to be in his house to talk to him, and I need to be in his house to talk to him uninterrupted, because if I'm at home I have the phone ringing and I have everybody's life to take care of. I have my poor mother's life to take care of and, again, my poor mother doesn't know how to defend herself. She doesn't know how to defend herself against her family, and she puts me in the awkward position to have to fight her battles. I have to stick up for her tell her family to push off and leave her alone, and if they deal with her they deal with me—and I'm dying.

I don't think my family has accepted the fact that I'm dying. I'm chronically, terminally ill, and I guess I've not accepted it. So if I've not accepted it, how can I expect my family to? All that I'm doing every day is making sure my business is in order; making sure that I don't have a lot of garbage to get rid of if I die; making sure that I don't make it hard on my husband to have to go through my junk and try to sort out the good from the bad; making sure that my sister, my ally, my best friend, my person that I can run to, knows what she has to take and sort through; where my insurance policies are at, where my will is at, where my do-not-resuscitate is at, and where my healthcare directives are at. But is equally important for me to tell my family how important it is for them to acknowledge that the people that were around me, that helped me, that they be friends with them, and that they acknowledge that they were a very important part of my growing up, my intricate part of being.

CHAPTER TWELVE

Back to selling cars … One of my best friends, Yolanda, and her brother owned a dealership. I learned to sell cars, but I quickly learned that selling cars was not for me. It's a guy's field; it's a man's job, because selling cars as a girl means that you're sitting passenger in a car with a strange guy that could hurt you, and, ironically, I put myself in that position. I was a young good-looking gal that was very top-heavy, and men sometimes looked at me the wrong way because I was top-heavy. I worked at AutoMax USA when I went on a test drive with a man who, halfway through the driving experience, decides to tell me that women like me make men like him inadequate, that we make enough money to where we make them feel like they're not an important part of our life, and how he needed to get rid. Well, I guess it turns out that either he was a rapist or a serial killer, or a combination of the two, and I just happened to be in his pathway.

He's in the driver seat; I'm in the passenger seat. My friend Yolanda's back at the dealership wondering why the test drive is not over in fifteen minutes, because the average test drive only took about fifteen minutes. We were supposed to get on the freeway off the Wapato exit, turn back around, get back onto the freeway, get back into the Yakama exit, and call the test drive over. This guy, that wasn't his plan. His plan was, I think and I believe wholeheartedly,

120

to rape me. My girlfriend I think knew that, and by the time we got back to the dealership she had already called the police, but before we got back to the dealership, he pulls over into an apple orchard and tells me what he is going to do to me. He tells me that he is going to rape me and leave me in the orchard and go back to the dealership, get into his car, and leave.

What he had not accounted for was my fight or flight and that he wasn't the first person to victimize me, nor the last, so I was ready for what was about to take place. I had my keys in my hand, so I knuckled up my hand and put the keys so that part of the keys were partially coming out of my knuckles of my gripped hand. I figured I had two shots. One was to try to scratch him in the face area or poke his eyes, or go for his jugular with these keys and hope that the keys did the job of hurting him enough to where I could run. I'm not sure where I thought I was going to run. I was going to run into the orchard, I guess, and fight for my life, but what actually took place was that I was able to talk to this guy in such a way that I scared him.

I quickly reminded him that everybody at the dealership knew that we were on a test drive. I quickly reminded him that he was on break from work, and I also quickly reminded him he had a wife and kids at home, and that, yes, he could rape me, and, yes, he could kill me, and, yes he could leave me out in this orchard, but he was not going to get away scot-free, because my family was going to find him. My brothers were going to find him. My girlfriend Yolanda was going to call the police, and she was going to tell her brother Frank that something was wrong, which she did.

By the time I came back to the dealership, Frank and Yolanda were both there ready to help me, and the police was there ready to question this man and took him, and he didn't rape me. He didn't even put a finger on me, but he scared the life out of me. What he made me see was that there's evil people in the world and you don't know who you're going to be faced with, up against, and that this person could be much stronger than you. and that you had to just trust your instinct. My instinct was to quit the auto business. I was not cut out for selling cars.

I was cut out for selling, but just not cars. That meant that I had to figure out something else to sell, which eventually landed me in the insurance business—but thank you, Yolanda. Thank you for looking out for me, girl. I know you're up in heaven, and I'm coming to visit with, and you and I have a lot to talk about. We have a lot to talk about, and sometimes stars are meant to shine in the sky, and maybe she was just meant to be a star. Maybe she was just meant to be for a small period of time, and then be gone and look down at us forever, take care of us, and help us out in some situations.

Maybe that's what my goal is. Maybe it's my job to look out for my mother and my family from someplace else other than here. But for as long as I'm here, it is my obligation, and it is my job, to look out for me, to care for me, to take care of that child that always took care of me, and that's me.

I have to look out for my granddaughter so that she is not a victim of this tradition, this loophole, that has taken place, so that my granddaughter will live her life to the max, and that she will go off and become a professional before she becomes a wife, before she becomes a mother. Then she will set the pace for my other granddaughters. She's not my only grandchild. She's just my first granddaughter that I feel can be a very important piece of the puzzle that makes me up. I've left her my wedding ring and my wedding dress so that she can wait till the day she gets married so that Nana can give her the gift, and she can give me the gift of marrying at the right time; not hurrying up to be married, not hurrying up to be an adult, but enjoying her preteen years, enjoying her teen years, enjoying her adult years, enjoying her adolescence, and enjoying her college years, enjoying relationships and boyfriends and friends and girlfriends, and everything that life has got to offer, so that she's not riddled with illness, premature death, premature sadness, and premature fears.

I want her to do things at the right pace, and I want my son to graduate from medical school. I want my older son to be a good father to his family, be a good husband to his wife, and I want my daughter to stick with her husband and teach her family stability, teach her husband that she has the makings of a great wife, and that he has the great makings of a great husband. When I'm gone, and when I'm no longer here to fend for them, I've done my job as a sister. I've done my job as a mother. I've done my job as a daughter, and I've done my job as a community member. I've taught my neighbors by example that it's all right to be a good neighbor. It's all right to groom your neighbor's yard if he or she can't do it. It's all right to open a door for an older person. It's all right to greet somebody with a smile on your face. It's all right to be happy. There's nothing wrong with being positive. If all you have to leave when you're gone is your energy, your positive nature, your optimism, your relentless inability to give up, if that's all you have to leave at the end of the day, bravo!

My last name is Bravo not by accident. My last name is Bravo because my father gave me that name, and because my father had predetermined me to be a strong, strong, fearless female. My last name is now Bravo-Cortines because I finally married a man that told me it's going to be all right, and although he's older than I, and wiser than I, he doesn't know more than I about a lot of things. He knows more than I about life because he's lived longer and he's had a greater opportunity of learning more than I have, and he had a better upbringing than I did. He was socially all right. He was a single child in a well-to-do home with a mom, dad, a stable background, great education, stable marriage—well, at least superficially stable—and a great career, but even in his sixties he's not sure that everything he's done has been correct. I'm in my forties, so I guess what it comes down to is I'm in my forties living a ninety-year-old life riddled with ninety-year-old aches and pains, but the knowledge of, I'm assuming, a sixty-year-old, based on life experience.

So matter how I slice or dice it, I'm older than my age. I'm just living in a smaller amount of youth and body and years, and it's all right. It's all right to be where I'm at. It's all right to have learned what I've learned, but it's also all right to have been my own therapist, even though I spoke with a therapist—and Anne has helped me a great deal through some of my stuff and some of my emotions. Thank you, Anne.

Again, thank you to everybody that has helped me. It's all right to have emotions. It's all right to be tough, but it's also all right to call it a day. If you're tired and you're sick and you're riddled with illness, it's all right to call it a day. You don't need somebody's permission, including your families', to call it a day, but I can't just fold up tent and go. I have to fight. I have to fight like a lion. I have to fight like a Taurus, because that's what I am, a full-blown Taurus. I have to fight, fight, fight, fight to live, fight to laugh, fight to find humor in being on life support.

I just got out of the hospital a week ago. I was on a feeding tube, and being on a feeding tube realizing that, oh my God, cancer is taking over me. The disease is taking over me. The chemo and the bios are taking over me, and my body is starting to give up. I've accepted death. I've accepted that this is what it is, and chalked it up to this is what it is. At the same time, I just like to think of my last name and think of what Bravo means. I'd like to dedicate my book, *Bravo*, to all my family, all my loved ones, all the people that have challenged me, but also all the people that encouraged me, and all the great people that I've met in my life, because this book has been twenty, thirty, forty years in the making. This book has been in the making before I was even in existence. This book was in the making vicariously through my mother, I guess, and through her experiences, and through my grandmother's experiences. What I've learned is that I come from a long line of very strong, very hardworking, very honest, very willed women, and that my family is going to do all right. Everybody will do all right.

I also dedicate this book to my husband, who has been a great support system. Even if I don't say it, thank you for being my husband, thank you for believing in me, and thank you for taking care of me. Thank you for loving me. Through thick and through thin, thank you for loving me, and thank you for accepting that forgiveness is who I am and that I don't hold any hostility towards anyone. Loving is what I do best, and taking care of my family is what I do best. It's crazy, but maybe that's what I was put here for, and maybe I've taken care of all that I can take care of. Now I just have to take care of me. I have to take care of Teresa Bravo. Again, thank you, everyone. Thank you for hearing me out, thank you for being a part of my journey, and thank you for being my friends. Thank you.

Review Requested:
If you loved this book, would you please provide a review at Amazon.com?

CPSIA information can be obtained
at www.ICGtesting.com
Printed in the USA
FSOW02n0754141016
26128FS

9 781681 816579